CULTURE SMART!
PERU

John Forrest and Julia Porturas

D1059570

This book is available for special discounts for bulk purchases for sales promotions or premiums. Special editions, including personalized covers, excerpts of existing books, and corporate imprints, can be created in large quantities for special needs.

For more information in the USA write to Special Markets/Premium Sales, 1745 Broadway, MD 6–2, New York, NY 10019, or e-mail specialmarkets@randomhouse.com.

In the United Kingdom contact Kuperard publishers at the address below.

ISBN 978 1 85733 667 2
This book is also available as an e-book: eISBN 978 1 85733 668 9
British Library Cataloguing in Publication Data
A CIP catalogue entry for this book is available from the British Library

First published in Great Britain 2006
by Kuperard, an imprint of Bravo Ltd
59 Hutton Grove, London N12 8DS
Tel: +44 (0) 20 8446 2440 Fax: +44 (0) 20 8446 2441
www.culturesmart.co.uk
Inquiries: sales@kuperard.co.uk

Distributed in the United States and Canada
by Random House Distribution Services
1745 Broadway, New York, NY 10019
Tel: +1 (212) 572-2844 Fax: +1 (212) 572-4961
Inquiries: csorders@randomhouse.com

Series Editor Geoffrey Chesler
Design Bobby Birchall

Printed in Malaysia

Cover image: *Traditional embroidered textile from Peru.* © iStockphoto.com

The photographs on pages 19, 50, 60, 65, 67, 70, 93, 102, 107, and 127, are reproduced by permission of John Forrest, and on page 131 by permission of Ana Maria Parodi Mathorel.

Images on the following pages reproduced under Creative Commons Attribution-Share Alike 3.0 Unported license: 28 © Håkan Svensson (Xauxa); 42, 90, 124 © AgainErick; 58 © Huhsunqu; 86 © Rodrigo.Argenton; 101, 138 © Manuel González Olaechea y Franco; 123 © EXPRESO CABANINO S.A ETECSA; 143 © WEBSTER1991

Reproduced under Creative Commons Attribution-Share Alike 2.0 Generic license: 56 © MattKingston; 95 © One Laptop Per Child

About the Authors

JOHN FORREST is a teacher and writer based in London. He first traveled to Peru in 1981, after graduating with a BA Comb.Hons in Geography and Statistics from Exeter University. He returned to Peru regularly to lead study tours and to research, write, and publish his own travel guide. He is a committee member of the Anglo-Peruvian Society and continues to visit Peru as Chairman of the Tambopata Reserve Society.

JULIA PORTURAS was born in Peru and studied at La Católica University in Lima and Birkbeck College, London. She graduated with a BA Hons in Hispanic and Latin American Studies. In Peru, she worked for several years for a major state enterprise, and she is now an administrator in London.

John and Julia are both contributors to Footprint's Peru guides.

**The Culture Smart! series is continuing to expand.
For further information and latest titles visit
www.culturesmart.co.uk**

The publishers would like to thank **CultureSmart!**Consulting for its help in researching and developing the concept for this series.

CultureSmart!Consulting creates tailor-made seminars and consultancy programs to meet a wide range of corporate, public-sector, and individual needs. Whether delivering courses on multicultural team building in the USA, preparing Chinese engineers for a posting in Europe, training call-center staff in India, or raising the awareness of police forces to the needs of diverse ethnic communities, it provides essential, practical, and powerful skills worldwide to an increasingly international workforce.

For details, visit www.culturesmartconsulting.com

CultureSmart!Consulting and **CultureSmart!** guides have both contributed to and featured regularly in the weekly travel program "Fast Track" on BBC World TV.

contents

contents

Map of Peru

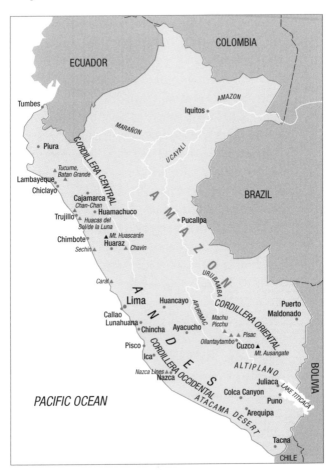

introduction

In the popular imagination, Peru conjures up images of mysterious ancient civilizations, awe-inspiring Inca cities, conquistadores risking all in their search for gold, spectacular Andean scenery, incredible biodiversity, and colorful woven textiles. There is much more to it than this.

Of all the South American countries Peru has the greatest variety of food and music, and the widest extremes of climate and landscape. It has the riddle of ancient lines in the desert, and modern-day intrigue and political scandal. Add to this potent mix the friendly nature of its people, and Peru is a country that has to be experienced!

This is a land of huge contradictions. It has plentiful natural resources, from which the majority of Peruvians derive relatively little benefit. It is a country that was the basis for the largest empire in the Americas, but which has seen nearly two hundred years of political chaos; a country with a long Pacific coastline, yet is half-covered with tropical rain forest; and that, until fifteen years ago, had only three tarmac roads up into the Andes.

Despite this inaccessibility the two distinctive cultures that first encountered each other five hundred years ago have, progressively, integrated. However, this mixing of races and cultures raises questions about the nature of Peruvian identity. Peruvian society is divided between the wealthy, Westernized coastal urban populations and the poorer, traditional indigenous peoples, many of whom have migrated from the Andes to the cities.

Most Peruvians are laid-back and surprisingly calm and carefree given the political, economic, and natural uncertainties they face. The Andean people are more fatalistic, but love to enjoy themselves at their numerous fiestas. Religious festivals, a blend of Catholic and pre-Columbian beliefs, also provide plenty of opportunity.

Peruvians are increasingly embracing consumerism, but for their happiness they still depend on each other, and the family is paramount. *Culture Smart! Peru* introduces you to the complex realities of modern Peruvian life. It describes how history and geography have helped to shape contemporary values and attitudes. The chapter on customs and traditions gives an insight into religious and public life, while others reveal what people are like at home, in business, and in their social life. Peruvians are outgoing and sociable, so the more effort you make to meet and understand them, the more you will find them welcoming, generous, and hospitable.

Key Facts

Official Name	República del Peru	
Capital City	Lima Population: 8 million	"The City of Kings," it was founded on Epiphany.
Main Cities	Arequipa, Trujillo, Chiclayo, Cuzco	
Area	494,208 sq. miles (1,279,999 sq. km)	Coastal length: 1,491.33 miles (2,400 km)
Geography	Peru lies within the tropics.	Long border with Brazil to the east, with Ecuador and Colombia to the north, Bolivia and Chile to the south
Terrain	Great diversity of landscapes running N–S in 3 zones: desert in the west, rugged mountains and plateaus down the center, jungle in the east	Over half of Peru is covered by the Amazon basin.
Climate	Hugely varied: Coastal desert very hot in summer, cooler in winter; very dry. Mountains cold and dry in winter, milder and wet in summer. Jungle hot and wet most of the year	
Population	Approx. 28.3 million	
Life Expectancy	Men: 68 years Women: 71 years	
Ethnic Make-up	45% Amerindian, 37% *Mestizo* (Amerindian/White), 15% White, 2.5% Afro-Peruvian	400+ ethnic groups identified in the Peruvian Amazon
Currency	Nuevo sol (100 centavos)	

GDP	US $8,500 per capita per annum (2008 est.)	
Language	Spanish and Quechua (official languages)	Aymara widely spoken in southern Andes. Many indigenous languages in the Amazon
Religion	90% Catholic 5% Protestant	
Literacy	88%	Slightly higher for men than women
Government	Federal Republic with an elected president serving a 5-year term	A single 120-seat legislative chamber
Media	Two quality national newspapers: *El Comercio* and *La República*. *Caretas* is a highly respected weekly magazine. Most cities publish a regional newspaper.	Canal N and America Television are the most informative channels. Otherwise dominated by *telenovelas* (soap operas). BBC/CNN available in urban areas
Media English Language	*Newsweek* and *Time* are available in Lima.	
Electricity	220 volts, 60 Hz A/C (Arequipa has 50 Hz)	European appliances need adaptors.
Video/TV	NTSC system	
Internet Domain	.pe	
Telephone	Country code: 51	Main cities have their own codes.
Time	GMT minus 5 hours	

chapter one

LAND & PEOPLE

GEOGRAPHICAL SNAPSHOT

The third largest country in South America, Peru is traversed north to south by the narrow Atacama desert in the west, the Andes mountains down the center, and Amazon rain forest in the east. It is bordered to the north by Ecuador and Colombia, to the east by Brazil, to the south by Bolivia and Chile, and to the west by the Pacific Ocean.

Peru is a Spanish-speaking country, though over a third of the people also speak Quechua, the indigenous language spoken widely but in a variety of dialects the length of the Andes. It has nearly 30 million inhabitants, 8.5 million of whom live in the sprawling capital, Lima.

There is a wealth of dramatic landscapes and in a day it is possible to travel from searing desert heat, through freezing high Andean fog, and down into the humid rain forest.

The Atacama desert, the driest in the world, extends northward from Chile almost to the Ecuadorian border. The cold Peru (or Humboldt) ocean current flowing northward from Antarctica up the west coast of South America ensures the coastal air masses are moisture free. The Atacama is only 50 miles (80 km) wide at its broadest point in the north and in places almost disappears as the Andean foothills reach down to the sea. It is crossed by narrow fertile valleys watered by fast-flowing rivers with sources high in the Andes.

The Andes result from millennia of tectonic activity as the oceanic Nazca plate is drawn beneath the continental South American plate. Consequently, the mountain ranges (*cordilleras*) are oldest toward the east and more recently formed near the coast. This leads to frequent earth tremors, though the last big earthquake was in 1970. Most volcanic activity is experienced in the south, where there are several active volcanoes and plenty of evidence of past eruptions.

In the south the Andes splits into two main *cordilleras* divided by a high-altitude, infertile plateau, the *altiplano* ("high plain"). It is on this plateau that Lake Titicaca, the world's highest navigable lake, is situated, at 12,600 feet

(3,850 meters) above sea level. Many rivers are
deeply incised into the lower flanks of the Andes,
most notably at Cotahuasi and Colca, near
Arequipa, the deepest canyons in the world.

The source of the Amazon lies high in the
Andes in central southern Peru: over half the
country is dense tropical rain forest through
which flow thousands of tributaries of the largest
river on the planet.

CLIMATE

Peru has three distinct climatic zones, though
there are significant seasonal variations within each.

Lima is shrouded in cloud for at least four
months of the year (July–October) and at times
"La Garúa," a sea mist, sweeps in at street level
between the hotels and apartment blocks. It can
feel surprisingly damp and chilly. By driving
12–18 miles (20–30 km) inland, however, it is
possible to leave all that behind and enter a
landscape of clear blue skies and almost
permanent sunshine and warmth.

In the Andes the weather can be extremely
changeable, especially when crossing the
cordilleras, so it may seem like summer one
moment and winter the next.

About every ten years Peru is affected by the
"El Niño" phenomenon. The northward flow of
the cold Humboldt Current is restricted by a
sudden surge of warmer water from across the
central Pacific. The accompanying warmer, moist

Climatic Zone	Summer (Nov–Apr)	Winter (May–Oct)
Coast (up to 19 miles/30 km inland)	Clear skies. Very hot. No rain	Very cloudy and cool in the south, broken skies and warmer in the north. No rain
Coastal strip (inland—foothills of the Andes)	Early mist disappears to leave clear skies. Very hot. No rain	Early mist disappears to leave clear skies. Warm. No rain
High Andes	Cloudy, warm, and wet	Clear skies, cool, and dry. At high altitudes very cold at night but warm in the day
Amazon	Cloudy, very warm, and very wet	Less cloudy, very warm, and wet, but at times in the south may not rain for a week. In a *friaje* (cold spell) temps. can drop to 54–59°F (12–15°C).

air brings cloud, rain, and strong winds to the northern desert. The opposite, but less frequent, "La Niña" brings much colder, drier weather to the southern Andes.

PERU'S DEPARTMENTS

Peru, a Federal Republic, is divided into twenty-four departments, subdivided into 195 provinces, which are further divided into 1,637 districts. In the 1990s eleven regions were created, most consisting of several departments.

The most densely populated departments are those along the coast, the most sparsely in the Amazon. In the 1980s and 1990s there was significant internal migration from Andean to coastal departments as a consequence of the civil war, with many coastal cities increasing rapidly and significantly in size. However, within coastal departments there are large uninhabited expanses of desert between coastal cities.

A BRIEF HISTORY

Modern Peru is a composite of populations and cultures, shaped by a series of remarkable historical events. These can only be covered in the briefest of detail here, but are central to an understanding of the Peruvian people.

Peru's pre-Columbian past ranks with that of other great ancient civilizations, evidenced by some spectacular archaeological discoveries. The impressive remains of the Inca dynasty, the most extensive civilization to flourish in the Americas, still have a tremendous physical and cultural impact on the lives of many Andean people.

After the conquest, Spain established its own empire across much of South America, with Peru at its heart. Spanish influence remains strong today, with some fine colonial-era buildings in the major cities. Following Peru's independence, Britain and then the USA had a major impact on the economy. In recent years globalization has seen a transfer of power to major transnational companies. None, however, have managed to diminish Peru's strong cultural identity.

Prehistory

The first signs of human habitation in Peru were unearthed in the central highlands and coastal *lomas* (vegetation surviving off the sea mist). They date back to 8,000–6,000 BCE. The people were seminomadic hunter-gatherers whose ancestors had probably crossed from Asia when the Bering Straits froze over and migrated down through the Americas (20,000–10,000 BCE).

Not everyone agrees with the Bering Straits theory about the land route taken by Peru's first peoples. The Norwegian Thor Heyerdahl, whose Kon-Tiki expeditions set sail from Peru, suggested an alternative, or additional, trans-Pacific migration. Strong mongoloid features—in support of this—as depicted in pre-Columbian ceramic figurines, can also be found today among the inhabitants of any town on the Peruvian north coast. Another theory promotes the peopling of Peru westward from the Amazon.

THE OLDEST CITY IN THE NEW WORLD

Recent archaeological discoveries at Caral, in the Supe valley 160 miles (260 km) north of Lima, have radically changed views about the origins and nature of early societies both within Peru and more universally. Caral, an extensive urban center, has been dated to 2600 BCE—far older than any other sizable site in the Americas. Furthermore, its principal function does not appear to have been military but trade related, which has overturned previously accepted theories about the origins of cities. Ceremonial platforms or *huacas*—a term used to describe sacred sites and objects, often large platform pyramids—also cover the site. It seems that at this time there were sufficient resources for communities not to need to take up arms against each other.

Caral is an indication that much more about the ancient history of Peru awaits discovery in the desert sands and coastal valleys.

Pre-Columbian Civilizations

The earliest inhabitants of Peru created numerous distinctive and fascinating cultures over many centuries. Variations in their chronology and geographical extent, the occupation of sites by more than one culture, plus ongoing discoveries, create difficulties in their classification. Most of them developed across several adjacent coastal or Andean valleys with probable trade links between the two zones. They conquered and assimilated each other, an approach at which the Incas were, ultimately, the most adept. When the Spanish arrived they found a well-organized, complex society but one that was incapable of offering significant resistance to European weaponry.

Pre-Ceramic Period (8000–1850 BCE)
On the coast plentiful seafood and game gradually encouraged occupation of the valleys as climatic change reduced the *lomas*. In the Andes the guanaco (wild Andean cameloid) was domesticated—to produce the larger llama and alpaca—as were guinea pigs. However, people continued to live in isolated hunter-gatherer groups, seasonally cultivating a few plants.

Initial Period (1800–800 BCE)
Increasing cultivation generated a food surplus that led to the appearance of a craftsman class devoted to basic metalworking, weaving, and, for the first time, pottery production. The stone rubble pyramid of Sechin Alto, in the Casma valley, 230 miles (370 km) north of Lima, dates to 1400 BCE, and was the largest structure in the Americas at the time.

Early Horizon (800–200 BCE)

Aside from Caral, it was the Andes that saw the beginnings of structured society within Peru. Chavin de Huantar, located immediately southeast of the Cordillera Blanca, and Sechin, due west of Chavin on the coast, became important religious and political centers.

Chavin was the focus of a quasi-religious cult that worshiped a feline creator god (suggesting close links with the rain forest). Its influence stretched hundreds of miles across northern Peru, from which pilgrims flocked to visit. The complexity of the cult is reflected in the quality of the ceramics and metalwork produced and in a stunning stone pyramid complex. The main pyramid has several levels of underground galleries, which terminate at finely sculptured stone monoliths decorated with feline and anthropomorphic forms.

Sechin consists of a temple platform faced with hundreds of carved stone monoliths. The carvings are remarkable for the clear depiction of a warrior society and an apparent narrative reflecting a violent lifestyle. The link with Chavin is unclear but Sechin may have acted as a military base to spread and maintain the cult.

The Chavin cult linked many disparate groups, from Paracas in the south to Kuntur Wasi (Cajamarca) in the north, despite the hostile nature of the intervening terrain. At Chavin significant advances were made in developing ceramic vessels, while at Paracas incredibly fine cotton textiles—best seen in the museums in Lima—were produced.

THE MYSTERIOUS NASCA LINES

The intriguing shapes etched into the desert just outside the towns of Nasca and Palpa originally consisted of numerous huge geometric designs and long lines crisscrossing  the desert. Toward the end of their construction period a series of anthropomorphic and zoomorphic drawings depicting, among others, a monkey, spider, hummingbird, and killer whale, were added to the Pampa (Plain) of San Jose. The Lines remain little altered to this day because only a light breeze ever blows across the Pampa, insufficient to disturb the dark pebbles, oxidized over millennia. The Lines were made by clearing the pebbles to reveal the paler sand beneath.

Theories abound as to the origins of the Lines but one thing is clear—they can only be satisfactorily viewed from above. Links to visiting aliens, ancient hot air balloon flights across the Pampa, and the reflection of an astronomical calendar have all been dismissed. The most widely accepted view is that different communities within the valley were responsible for different lines and drawings. The individual designs relate to the shamanic beliefs of each group and to the shaman's ability to "fly" once he has entered the spirit world. The creation and maintenance of the Lines was undertaken by community members during rituals in which offerings were made to the gods to ensure availability of water and fertility of the land. The Lines can be observed from a viewing tower just outside Nasca, and by plane— flights, lasting one hour, take off from the small airport.

Early Intermediate Period (200 BCE–600 CE)
This was a period of rapid change in which significant technological developments in metalworking, pottery, and weaving took place in several coastal valleys. Two of the most interesting are the Nasca and Mochica cultures.

Several Nasca culture communities, 5,000 to 10,000 strong, lived in the Nasca valley, 250 miles (400 km) south of Lima. They were responsible for the construction of highly sophisticated underground irrigation systems, a large number of ceremonial sites, and the Nasca Lines, and produced highly decorative pottery.

Mochica culture was based in the Moche valley (Trujillo), 350 miles (560 km) north of Lima. The Mochica developed a military state that extended from the Casma valley, in the south, to the Chira valley (Piura), in the north. Extensive irrigation of the coastal valleys supported a craftsman class that produced exquisite jewelry and stylized, though amazingly lifelike, portrait ceramics of people, animals, and common foods, revealing a huge amount about the daily life of the Mochica. Pottery decoration also indicates that they sailed and traded along the coast from balsa log vessels.

The enormous Huaca del Sol (Pyramid of the Sun) and Huaca de la Luna (Pyramid of the Moon) with its brightly painted interior frescos—adjacent to each other just outside Trujillo—are fantastic monuments to the culture, as is the mysterious fresco-covered Huaca del Brujo (Pyramid of the Witches) further up the coast. The "royal" Mochica tomb of El Señor de Sipan (near Chiclayo), with its beautiful golden and silver treasures, is another legacy. All these constructions demonstrate a capacity to organize large-scale community participation, over many years, in building projects.

Middle Horizon (600–1000)
As the Nasca and Mochica cultures waned, quite possibly as a result of "El Niño" related events, the Huari-Tiahuanaco culture came to the fore in the southern Andes. The military skills of the Huari

(at Ayacucho) combined with the existing religious cult of Tiahuanaco (southern end of Lake Titicaca) to create the first great pan-Andean empire. At its height it extended from Cajamarca, in the north, to northern Bolivia and Argentina, in the south.

The Huari were the first to construct large walled settlements—for example, Piquillacta, outside Cuzco, and Cajamarquilla, outside Lima—recognizable roads, and extensive terraces on the steep Andean hillsides. Their empire was controlled by well-run labor and administrative systems until it eventually fragmented.

Lambayeque (Sican) culture flourished around 750–1350 CE. After the collapse of the main Mochica culture, a northern group reestablished itself in the Lambayeque and surrounding valleys, beyond the influence of the Huari. They were responsible for constructing the impressive site of Batan Grande, dotted with huge adobe pyramids, including Huaca Loro (Parrot Pyramid), from which amazing golden and copper treasures were unearthed in the tomb of El Señor de Sican (The Lord of Sican). Climatic change led to the building of a new site, a short distance west at Tucume, where Huaca Larga (Long Pyramid) is the biggest adobe structure in the world. The culture survived until conquered by the Chimu.

Late Intermediate (1000–1470)

With the demise of the Huari in the south two major cultures appeared in northern Peru. The Chachapoyans took control in the Andes from their citadel at Kuelap, while, on the coast, the Chimu culture (900–1470) appeared in the Moche valley and later conquered (1350) the Lambayeque valley. In the Moche valley they constructed Chan-Chan, the largest adobe city ever built; covering 8 sq. miles (20 sq. km), it was larger than any subsequent Inca city. In the Lambayeque valley they took over and expanded existing Sican structures. A highly organized, militaristic state, it was contemporary with the early Inca empire.

Late Horizon (1400–1532)
Much uncertainty surrounds the origins of the Incas (c. 1200–1532). The two most commonly told legends have Manco Capac and Mama Ocllo, his sister, coming from an island on Lake Titicaca in about 1200 CE, while another states that they and their brothers emerged from caves north of the lake. They were the creation of Viracocha—the creator god—and the  children of the Sun (Inti, another deity) on earth. In reality they were probably a small tribal grouping displaced from the periphery of Lake Titicaca. Their initial wanderings led them to a fertile valley where Manco Capac's staff sank into the ground, and Cuzco was founded.

TYING UP THE SUN

The Incas appear to have believed in a single creator, Viracocha, who was responsible for the creation of numerous other deities, of which the Sun was the most important—more significant than Viracocha in terms of daily worship as reflected in the building of temples of the Sun throughout the empire.

The principal temple of the Sun was Qoricancha, in Cuzco, which housed huge golden disks representing the sun and life-sized golden and silver sculptures adorning the patios. At the end of each day it is believed that priests coordinated a ritual in which the sun was ceremonially tied to the Intihuatana (Hitching Post of the Sun, a four-cornered stone) to ensure that it would return the next day. The Moon, Stars, Earth (Pachamama), Rainbows, Thunder, Water, and Mountains (apus) were some of the other components of the Incas' religious cosmology.

The ruler, the Inca, was revered like a deity, lived like a king, and on death his body was mummified and retained for ancestor worship. He was attended by the Acllas (Virgins of the Sun), wore only the finest clothes, and then only once, while all his food was tasted for poison by a servant.

Successive Inca rulers, most notably Pachacutec (1438–71) and Tupac Inca (1471–93), extended the Inca empire (Tahuantisuyo) until it became the largest ever in the Americas. At its zenith it ran the length of the Andes from present-day southern Colombia to the Maule valley, in central Chile. Cuzco, the "navel of the universe," lay at the heart of Tahuantisuyo, which was subdivided into four regions: Chinchaysuyo, to the north; Antisuyo, to the east; Contisuyo, to the southwest; and Collasuyo, to the southeast.

The key to the establishment of the Inca dynasty was their ability to impose their ideology on conquered peoples, whose skills they integrated and assimilated. Conquered tribes were wholly, or partially, dispersed around the empire to nullify any further threat, in a practice known as *mitimae*. Consequently, the specialist skills they possessed— stonecutting or weaving, for example—were also transferred, as was the Quechua language. The Incas demanded that citizens, in huge numbers, form militias and undertake public works through a "tax" system known as *mit'a*. This arrangement was responsible for the highly ambitious construction projects, ranging from lengthy highways to great palaces and citadels. With limited tools, huge blocks of stone were cut to fit together perfectly without the use of mortar. Such expertise allowed the Incas to build spectacular defensive and ceremonial sites, principally in the Cuzco area, such as the fort of Sacsahuaman above the city and, in the Sacred Valley, Pisaq, Ollantaytambo, and Machu Picchu.

One of the most remarkable aspects of Inca achievements was that everything was undertaken in the absence of a written language, the wheel, or

horses. Records were kept using a system of knotted strings (*quipus*—the origin of modern-day bar codes), while all communication was made through a series of runners (*chasquis*), with small loads transported by llamas.

The Conquest

In 1527 the Inca, Huayna Capac, died of smallpox—a disease brought to the Americas by the Spanish that had spread south ahead of the *conquistadores'* arrival. In an unprecedented move Huayna Capac had divided the Inca empire, giving his legitimate son Huascar control of Cuzco and the south, while his half-brother Atahualpa was placed in charge of Chinchaysuyo, from Quito. Civil war erupted, with Atahualpa defeating Huascar at Cajamarca in 1532.

Concurrent with the upheavals in the Inca empire a group of licensed adventurers from Extremadura in western Spain—led by Francisco

Pizarro and his brothers—ventured from Panama down the west coast of South America. In one famous incident, on an island off the Ecuadorian coast, Francisco Pizarro challenged those with him to step over a line he drew in the sand and continue south into the unknown in search of fame and fortune. Only a handful chose to do so.

On their third expedition they finally landed on the north coast of Peru, near Tumbes. Demonstrating incredible courage and audacity, the tiny contingent (168 *conquistadores*, only 62 of whom were mounted) moved up into the Andes, encountered Atahualpa resting with his army of thousands near Cajamarca, and immediately took him captive. The Incas, who had never seen firearms and, initially, believed each Spanish horse and its rider to be a single creature, were too dumbfounded to resist. After securing a ransom room full of gold and silver the Spanish executed Atahualpa and marched on Cuzco. Crossing the difficult, hostile terrain at remarkable speed they were welcomed on arrival by Huascar's followers but proceeded to sack the city. The Incas could never have anticipated the Spanish greed for gold, or the death and destruction they were prepared to mete out to acquire wealth.

In 1535 Pizarro founded Lima-Callao for trading purposes, principally the shipment of gold, silver, and other treasures stripped from Peru back to the

Church and monarchy in Spain. However, while the Pizarros were accumulating great wealth, a fellow *conquistador*—Diego de Almagro—found no such riches in Chile. Lacking a share of the spoils Almagro turned on his former comrades. The argument culminated in the battle of Las Salinas, outside Cuzco, in which Almagro was captured and executed. Almagro's son killed Pizarro three years later, in 1541. In the meantime, Manco Inca—the Spanish-appointed "puppet" Inca—organized an uprising and besieged Cuzco. The Spanish force was almost eliminated but a handful of *conquistadores* held out and retook the fortress of Sacsahuaman above Cuzco from thousands of Inca warriors in a daring cavalry charge. Not for the first time a large Inca army, that only a few years before had been all-conquering, became disorganized and ineffective in the face of Spanish weaponry.

Spanish soldiers continued to be ambushed in subsequent years but, gradually, under Gonzalo Pizarro the Inca populace was subjugated. Only Manco Inca and a small band held out at Vilcabamba—in the rain forest beyond Machu Picchu—until hunted down and killed in 1544.

Colonial Peru

From the 1540s the Spanish monarchy ruled through the appointment of viceroys. Vilcabamba was infiltrated and overrun in 1572 and the last Inca—Tupac Amaru—killed. Spain imposed tribute and forced labor on the indigenous population to maximize agricultural and mining output:

hundreds of thousands died from exploitation and disease. Only once, in 1780–82, did an Inca noble of mixed blood, Tupac Amaru II, attempt an uprising, but it was quickly and brutally suppressed.

During this period Peru lay at the heart of the Spanish empire in South America. Schools and towns were founded; wheat, vines, olives, and European domestic animals were introduced. Trade was undertaken, primarily, to the benefit of the monarchy and the Church. Amazingly, all goods destined for Spain had to pass through Lima and, subsequently, Panama, including those originating in Argentina and Chile. Later Peru was divided into two administrative areas: Peru (modern Peru) and Upper Peru (modern Bolivia). Black slaves were brought in to work on the expanding coastal sugar plantations.

Independence

Dissatisfaction with colonial rule, once the Royalists regained power from Napoleon in Spain, combined with the rise of independence movements elsewhere in South America to encourage many Peruvians to consider self-government. The *criollos* (Creoles, Peruvians of direct Spanish descent) had long been shut out from all important positions. They had grown enormously wealthy from the vast *haciendas* and mines that, ostensibly, they ran for Spain's benefit. Now they and mixed-blood *mestizos* had a common cause. The opportunity arose in 1820, when the rebel Argentinian General José de San Martin landed at Paracas with a force from

Chile, while General Simón Bolivar and Marshal
Antonio de Sucre brought reinforcements south
from Colombia. Independence was declared at
Lima on July 28, 1821, but the Spanish army fled
to the *sierra* where it held out until its final defeat
at the battles of Junin and Ayacucho, in 1824.

San Martin and his supporters wanted to import
a European monarch as head of state, while Bolivar
planned to integrate Peru and Bolivia into his new
confederacy—Gran Colombia—but both plans
were rejected by the Peruvian liberals. In the years
after independence chaos reigned as one faction
took power and then another; presidents lasted only
a year or two, were ousted, took control of Bolivia,
and then returned again as president of Peru. In the
forty-five years following independence Peru had
thirty-four presidents, three at once at one point,
twenty-seven of whom were military men. In this
era only Ramon Castilla stood out as a unifying
president.

Peru's economic prospects picked up, however, with the growing demand in Europe for *guano* (bird droppings) fertilizer. Chinese migrants were brought in to mine the *guano* from coastal islands in appalling conditions. *Guano* income paid for the construction of the central and southern railways into the interior and other major infrastructure projects. Nevertheless, by the time the first true civilian president, Manuel Pardo, was elected (1872) the industry was in decline.

War of the Pacific

In 1879 Chile invaded Bolivia's coastal provinces, seizing control of its nitrate mines and leaving Bolivia landlocked. A mutual defense pact was invoked and Peru found itself at war with Chile. Chilean forces quickly occupied southern Peru as far north as Lima, including three nitrate-rich southern departments. Lima was pillaged. Peru's forces were defeated at Huamachuco and the country was forced into submission, something that still leaves a bitter taste in Peruvian mouths to this day.

Eventually, in 1883, General Iglesias signed the Treaty of Ancon, which acceded to most of Chile's demands, including the loss of the three southern departments—only Tacna was regained forty years later. Iglesias attempted to rule as a Chilean "puppet," while General Cáceres ("*el demonio de los Andes*"— the demon of the Andes) maintained resistance in the highlands until, in 1886, he seized the presidency with popular support and expelled the Chileans.

In 1889 Cáceres was forced to sign the Grace-Donoughmore Contract to settle Peru's international debts, but this left the ports, railways, fledgling rubber industry, and many other economic interests in the hands of British companies. Peru was a British "colony" in all but name: the railways were managed by a British company until 1963.

HEROES IMMORTALIZED

Whether on banknotes or in street names, the military leaders who performed heroically against the Chileans live on over a hundred years later. General Bolognesi put up great resistance despite the defeat of the land forces, while Alfonso Ugarte rode over the cliffs to his death rather than surrender the Peruvian standard.

Arguably, it's Admiral Miguel Grau who is the best remembered and, with his large bushy mustache, the most recognizable. As captain of Peru's only warship, the tiny *Monitor Huascar*, he fought against overwhelming odds and was killed before the capture of the vessel.

Recent History

For much of the twentieth century presidencies were characterized by periods of dictatorial rule. In the main, political and economic power remained in the hands of the oligarchy that had seized power at independence. Investments were made in the education, health, and transportation sectors, but chiefly in Lima and towns serving the vast agricultural estates of the coastal valleys. The interior was largely ignored, apart from where there were rich mining deposits. The indigenous people of the *sierra*, Black and Chinese

migrants, and an increasing number of *mestizos* grew into a large deprived underclass. Among the international community a saying arose that "Peru is a beggar sitting on a throne of gold."

Military influence grew in strength after the Second World War and in 1943–56, 1963, and 1968–80 the presidency was again occupied by generals. Their political leanings were center-left, nationalist, and populist, following the example of General Juan Perón in Argentina. The most radical in his approach was General Juan Velasco (1968–75), who formed close political and economic ties with the Soviet Union. He embarked on a progressive program of land reform and the nationalization of many foreign-owned companies, especially oil and mining enterprises. Western goods and culture were, in effect, banned—for example, only vehicles from Eastern bloc countries were imported and it was almost impossible to find Western music, perfumes, and clothing until the late 1970s.

By 1980, in line with world opinion, Peruvians were eager for a return to democracy. Fernando Belaunde Terry, an architect and previous president (1963–68), was reelected. However, during the elections a small bomb outside a polling station was the first sign that the country was about to go through more than a decade of horror that would rapidly change Peruvian society for good.

"Shining Path"

The regimes of Belaunde (1980–85) and Alan Garcia (1985–90) were not only beset by problems resulting from world economic recession, but by a bloody internal conflict, termed a "civil war" by many, that raged into the early 1990s. In all 60,000 are believed to have died, deaths that can be almost equally attributed to the military and two guerrilla movements: Sendero Luminoso ("Shining Path") and, to a lesser extent, the MRTA (Movimiento Revolucionario Tupac Amaru).

The development of both groups occurred in the *sierra*: Sendero in Ayacucho and the MRTA in San Martin and Junin, some of the poorest departments, neglected by successive presidents. The philosophy of Sendero and its leader, Abimael Guzman (a university philosophy professor) drew on the ideology of Chairman Mao and advocated the total destruction of the state along with much of its infrastructure. It involved the complete restructuring of society, the resurrection of many aspects of the Inca social order and systems, and a rejection of capitalism. But their methods included wanton killings and destruction that were soon matched by the increasingly desperate military authorities. Caught up in the middle of it all were thousands of poorly educated *campesinos* (peasant farmers). In many cases their only option was to flee and

thousands did, principally to Lima. By the late 1980s Sendero was active in Lima's shantytowns and almost the whole country was under a state of emergency.

In areas where Sendero was not active the more ideologically driven MRTA filled the vacuum with almost equal brutality. Eventually Lima was placed under curfew, trust between people was almost lost, and bomb attacks hit at the heart of government.

Finally, in 1992 Guzman was captured and imprisoned. In 1994–95 an amnesty offering lighter sentences for repentance, and a Truth Commission (report published in 2004), began to try to heal some of the wounds of the previous decade.

Toward the end of the 1980s economic recession was hitting the Garcia government as much as the struggle against Sendero. Garcia, Peru's youngest ever president, was a charismatic figure and a great orator—for some he was a potential leader of the less developed world—but when he tried to limit debt repayments to the IMF and foreign banks it backfired and international credit was cut off. Consequently, Garcia attempted to nationalize the banks, sending tanks through the front doors of some, but this only led to hyperinflation and economic collapse. Not only was Garcia and his party (APRA) discredited in the eyes of many, but so were politics in general.

APRA—POLITICAL SURVIVOR

Inspired by the Mexican and Russian revolutions, indigenous culture, and the writings of Carlos Jose Mariategui, Raul Haya de la Torre founded the Alianza Popular para la Revolución Americana while in exile in Mexico in the mid-1920s. His vision was one of a united Americas, devoid of class divisions and functioning through worker cooperatives. He returned to Peru to implement his ideas. In 1932, however, an uprising in Trujillo—APRA's power base—against working conditions on the sugar plantations was suppressed by the military, leaving several hundred workers dead. For fifty years suspicion and animosity remained strong between the two sides. No APRA candidate was able to assume the presidency until the election of Alan Garcia in 1985. APRA has endured into the twenty-first century due to its tight political structure and northern power base, while the fortunes of most other traditional political parties have declined dramatically.

The Fujimori Era

In the 1990 elections the population rejected the traditional political parties and elected a virtual unknown—Alberto Fujimori, a university rector of Japanese descent—instead of the novelist Mario Vargas Llosa. Nicknamed "El Chino," Fujimori didn't need to worry about past decades of maladministration and corruption that plagued other candidates and parties.

He immediately imposed a series of severe economic policies, not dissimilar to those publicly proposed by Vargas Llosa, to try to kick-start the economy. These measures, known as the "Fujishock," hit the ordinary citizen hard: many again lost their meager life savings. As Fujimori embarked on a series of liberalizing measures, including the privatization of almost all state industries, there was widespread opposition from the political establishment. Consequently, in April 1992 he dismissed Congress and the Supreme Court and assumed dictatorial powers with the support of the military. Despite this he remained popular with the masses, by slashing inflation, settling a fifty-year-old border dispute with Ecuador, arresting the guerrilla leaders, and clearly understanding how to manipulate the media, which frequently portrayed him assisting the victims of landslides or "El Niño." The mastermind behind the President was not his wife—who accused him of corruption, divorced him, and ultimately went on a hunger strike when she was prevented from running against him—but the shady figure of Vladimiro Montesinos.

The strange relationship between the President and the cashiered army officer turned lawyer must rank as one of the most remarkable political double acts ever. For the first few years of the presidency, Montesinos was almost never seen in public. By the mid-1990s, however, it was clear that he was exerting considerable influence over the regime. While inflation remained low, with Sendero in decline and standards of living rising slowly, there was only limited opposition. Perez de Cuellar, the ex-UN Secretary General, was easily defeated in the 1995 presidential election.

In 1996 the MRTA seized five hundred dignitaries, including government ministers, at a party at the Japanese embassy. After four months of stalemate and despite the release of most of the hostages, the army stormed the embassy freeing the remaining hostages but killing all the terrorists.

On the back of the siege success, Fujimori, despite a series of accusations and scandals, forced through constitutional changes allowing him to run for an unprecedented third term in 2000. Subsequent to a narrow victory, further revelations led to his downfall and flight to Japan. It was then revealed that Fujimori had been born in Japan and had never been constitutionally eligible to run for the Peruvian presidency.'

By then Montesinos had already fled Peru, on a yacht, and disappeared. Rumors abounded as to his whereabouts, crystallizing around the possibility that he had escaped to Venezuela for facial plastic surgery. After several months he was arrested there looking much the same—short, balding, and bespectacled. In 2008 Montesinos was found guilty and sentenced to a lengthy prison term. Fujimori was arrested in Chile in late 2005 and transferred to Peru. After a three-year trial he was found guilty, in 2009, and sentenced to twenty-five years in prison.

GOVERNMENT TODAY

Following Fujimori's flight the 2000 elections were rerun and his defeated opponent, Alejandro Toledo, emerged the victor. Born in a remote Andean village, he worked as a shoe-shine boy but went on to study and lecture at Stanford University. Like Fujimori he did not have the backing of an established party but enjoyed the support of the masses. His presidency was characterized by a lack of dynamism, minor scandals, and the continued growth and influence of transnational companies.

Toledo failed to inspire confidence as an independent newcomer, while the established political parties struggled to regain public trust. However, in the 2006 elections a notable political comeback was achieved by Alan Garcia (APRA), the former president (1985–90). Unlike the leftist, anti-American approaches of his near neighbors, Garcia was forced to make alliances with right-wing parties to obtain a majority in Congress. He was transnational company friendly, which led to economic benefits. However, the signing of a free trade agreement with the USA threatens greater exploitation in Amazonia, and the prospect of conflict with numerous indigenous groups.

In the 2011 presidential elections, Ollanta Humala, an unsuccessful candidate in the 2006 election, defeated Keiko Fujimori, the daughter of

the disgraced ex-president, in a second round of voting. During the run-in the right-leaning Keiko was favorite, with many suspicious of the former army officer, previously linked with the populist regime of Hugo Chavez in Venezuela. However, once Humala associated himself with President Lula in Brazil, and details of Keiko's links with her father's old regime leaked out, public opinion switched.

It was assisted by an outspoken attack by Vargas Llosa and numerous other intellectuals, persuading the public not to vote for Keiko. However, *Fujimoristas* retain significant influence and remain the second largest group in Congress.

Once in office Humala ditched the "grand transformation," including the nationalization of several industries, promised in his election campaign, though he has retained some of the social programs. Instead he has maintained the export-led, market-orientated economic model of his predecessors, which has continued to enable Peru to buck the global trend with respect to economic growth. However, he is trying to regulate illegal mining activities, their operating practices and impact on the environment. This has lead to serious clashes between the police and miners in several Andean and Amazon regions such as Madre de Dios.

The president is elected every five years; an incumbent may only run for reelection once. If no candidate secures over 50 percent in the first round, a second round is held between the top two candidates. At the same time congressional and regional elections are held, the former, for the 120-seat Congress, on a "first past the post" basis. Mayoral and municipal elections are held every four years. Town councils are run by the mayor and a prefect appointed by the government.

THE BUSINESS LANDSCAPE

The core of Peru's economy remains rooted in agriculture and the extractive sector. The limited manufacturing sector, principally located in Lima, is closely linked to the processing of these resources. In recent years tourism has brought new business possibilities.

The heavily irrigated coastal valleys are dominated by sugar cane, cotton, and, in the north, rice cultivation. The vast Chavi-mochic project, near Trujillo, has turned the desert green with export crops such as asparagus, avocados, oranges, grapes, and mangoes. The nitrate deposits of the south coast are long exhausted but oil is still obtained from ancient wells in the far north. In the *sierra* mining operations have proliferated recently, with huge mines extracting copper, silver, gold, or zinc.

In the rain forest small-scale alluvial gold is found along some rivers, while there are extensive oil deposits in the north. Exploration continues along the eastern flank of the Andes for new oil and gas deposits. In 2004, the enormous Camisea natural gas field, in the central rain forest, came on stream. Its reserves are large enough to supply Peru's energy needs for decades. There is great optimism about the benefits it will bring to industry and employment as energy prices stabilize. Many vehicles have converted to natural gas by installing a large canister in the trunk, to keep running costs down.

Tropical timbers such as mahogany have been extensively logged. Loggers now have to venture several weeks upriver; in the case of Madre de Dios this takes them into contact with isolated indigenous people and conflict is a possibility. Such is the shortage of mahogany that an international moratorium controls its export.

Lima-Callao handles the majority of imports and exports, and contains most of the major manufacturing and processing plants. Within Lima there are industrial corridors between Callao and central Lima, and along the Panamerican and central highways. There are two main business districts: downtown Lima, though this is declining, and San Isidro; there are also smaller commercial centers in many districts.

Tourism is increasingly important. There were more than two million visitors in 2010, including business travelers. However, most tourists visit only half a dozen well-known sites, and the challenge for the government is to develop the tourism infrastructure elsewhere.

In all business sectors, especially following the privatization of the 1990s, transnational companies now dominate. They have been especially active in the mining sector. Chileans are active in retail and tourism, while Chinese companies are increasingly entering the marketplace.

Peru is a founding member, in 1969, of the Andean Community (CAN), which aims to boost development and trade. It is also an associate member of MercoSur, formed in 1991 by Argentina, Uruguay, Chile, and Brazil. In 2008 Peru joined the Union of South American Nations (UNASUR), a new organization modeled on the European Union, which aims to absorb CAN and Mercosur. A single market for non-sensitive products will be created by 2014, and for sensitive products by 2019. In the long-term the intention is also to introduce a South American passport and currency, as well as common foreign, defence and energy policies among others.

In the last five years, Peru has signed free trade agreements with the USA and China, while negotiations with the EU are close to completion. Almost all trade is now conducted on preferential terms. The value of international trade, both imports and exports, has increased sixfold in the last ten years.

chapter two

VALUES &
ATTITUDES

It is difficult to generalize about values and
attitudes within Peru. Tremendous variations exist
between the lives of city dwellers and those in
rural areas, and between the "modern" coastal
compared to the "isolated" *sierra* and jungle
regions. Furthermore, there is great disparity
between the poor—over 50 percent of the
population live in poverty—and the rich—about
5 percent of the population are extremely wealthy.

RELIGION

One unifying factor between all these areas and
people of all backgrounds and circumstances is the
Roman Catholic Church. For three centuries the
Spanish authorities governing Peru ensured that
a legacy of their presence would be a devoutly
Catholic populace. Adherence to the Catholic
doctrine was (and is) essential to achieve social
acceptance and advancement, especially in the
political arena. Many Peruvians are fervent
believers and churches are full at Sunday mass.

At the time of the Conquest the religious
emissaries had to adopt a pragmatic approach to

convince indigenous people to switch their allegiance from their long-held beliefs. They built churches on top of significant Inca buildings, the best example being the construction of the church of Santo Domingo on the ruins of Qoricancha (Temple of the Sun) in Cuzco. Some indigenous beliefs were similar to those of Catholicism and could be adapted, such as the worship of a creator god, Viracocha. Peruvian Catholicism follows the syncretism found throughout Latin America, in which indigenous religious rituals have been integrated with Christian festivals, especially in the *sierra*: the Lord of the Earthquakes festival (see page 66), for example.

Catholicism permeates life from an early age through the family, the community, and schooling. It provides a structure to people's lives and spiritual support in dealing with poverty and the risks of natural hazards. Life is tough for most people and the Church provides guidance and comfort in times of need—a frequent requirement—including the framework of moral values with the family at its core. However, a declining respect among some sections of society has lead to the increased theft of sacred artifacts from many churches and sanctuaries.

While the Catholic Church retains great support, over the last decade the Evangelical churches have grown in number. In any *barrio* (neighborhood) there will be a scattering of small chapels—Adventistas (Adventists), Testigos de Jehova (Jehovah's Witnesses), to name two—with rudimentary fittings, and a handful of worshipers.

LIBERATION THEOLOGY

In the 1960s a group of Catholic priests working in some of the poorest districts of Latin American cities, such as Gustavo Gutiérrez in Lima, developed an alternative understanding of the role of the Church as working with the poor and those experiencing social injustice. Liberation theology promotes the idea of Christian community in action, in which the Church assists in liberating the poor by responding to local needs and not simply applying "Western" doctrines or being concerned only with people's spiritual needs. Liberation theology has now reached a much wider audience and has been adopted by many groups on other continents, though recognition by Rome itself remains limited.

LIVING FOR THE MOMENT

The fragility of life, the reality of never knowing what may lie around the corner, has a major impact on the lives of most Peruvians. In the past high inflation meant that salaries were worth progressively less as the month passed, which encouraged a spending culture. Many employees requested advances while their salaries still retained their value, which they would then spend, incurring debt and ending up living beyond their means. This practice continues despite greater economic stability through the growing use of store and credit cards. Many stores only offer big discounts to store cardholders making multiple purchases, while most credit cards apply a monthly service charge. Consequently, most Peruvians are on a roller-coaster ride between optimism as the economy recovers or a new president is elected, and pessimism as the economy or the president fail yet again.

The Andean peoples, in particular, tend to have a more fatalistic approach to life, a legacy of the servitude, disease, and wars that killed many thousands in the past. These may no longer be a threat today but many still struggle to survive and live a "normal" life.

Whatever the economic situation, many Peruvians have a hedonistic streak and love to enjoy themselves when the opportunity arises— during weekends and holiday periods—by having a party, making a trip, or dining out.

THE FAMILY
The Peruvian family is usually large and life revolves around it. Until the 1970s families with

eight to ten children were not uncommon, even fifteen, but nowadays two or three children are increasingly the norm. "Family" signifies all members of the family, from grandparents to uncles and aunts, as well as nonfamily godparents, who will expect to be included in all family events. The elderly are very much included and are respected by younger generations—there is little "ageism." Grandparents will always sit at the head of the table and for them grandchildren may be prepared to do something in the house.

Family members rarely choose to live far apart and the home is often extended to accommodate a son or daughter upon marriage. If this isn't possible they will live just a few blocks away from one parent or the other. It is rare for young adults to move away from their parents to live alone. For many couples it is often a struggle to "leave the nest" and they may stop in for a meal, given that they cannot yet afford a *muchacha* (maid).

GENDER ROLES

Peru is, unquestionably, a macho society in many ways, but at home it is the mother who rules the roost. This reflects a continuation of traditional roles in that the menfolk are the principal breadwinners while women are in charge of the home, and therefore the family. Peruvian women are very houseproud and homes that may appear neglected from the outside are usually sparkling indoors, while freshly washed clothes appear out on the line each day. Daughters help around the house but sons are expected to do so only occasionally and husbands less so, though changes are occurring in some families.

One area in which Peruvian women dominate is in the market. It is rare to see a man running a market stall. These are presided over by formidable-looking ladies with persistent sales techniques.

The average age of marriage has risen significantly in recent years and many couples are now choosing not to marry. Divorce is becoming less of a taboo but it is still greatly frowned upon, and for military personnel severely restricts promotion prospects, so many couples live separate lives or maintain unhappy "show" marriages. Having a child out of wedlock has become more socially acceptable, but many couples choose to marry early in the pregnancy. A first marriage in a Catholic church means that only a civil ceremony is possible if they marry again. Fathers are legally obliged to support children born out of wedlock. Abortions are illegal as Catholic values hold firm, but might be permitted on medical grounds. An expensive clinic is sometimes the answer.

SOCIAL TIES

Peruvians have many friends and usually look to turn regular acquaintances into stronger friendships. This is great news for the visitor because, given their love of hospitality, you will quickly find yourself invited out for a meal or to their homes, and to meet the family. If the friendship blossoms then you are likely to acquire the status of a brother or sister and be treated almost as a full family member.

The future of their children is paramount to most Peruvians. Foreign friends are often asked to become the "godfather" (*padrino*) of one of their children. *Padrinos* are expected to send gifts for birthdays and at Christmas, and to maintain an interest in their godchild's well-being. This could include help with their education.

Peruvians have busy social lives between work commitments, the immediate family, other relatives, and friends. When new friends are made it is usually through the workplace, or possibly a club, with people of a similar background. For foreigners there are fewer boundaries and you could just as easily make friends with someone from a very privileged as from a relatively ordinary background.

In small Andean communities the traditional pre-Hispanic *ayllu* principals of community cooperation still prevail, in which members of the community all come together to build a house for newly weds, gather in the harvest, or clean irrigation channels. In larger villages where there is more than one *ayllu*, local fiestas are celebrated within each *ayllu* and there is a degree of competition between them.

PRIDE, HONOR, AND *MACHISMO*

As with many Latin societies there is a strange dichotomy between *machismo* in the wider society and respect, even reverence, for the Virgin Mary and for all that the mother says and does at home.

Machismo is reflected, in most cases, through the husband setting his own agenda and, for example, going for a drink with friends and returning home whenever he pleases. It is also not uncommon for this to involve an extramarital relationship. A contributory factor to this is the nature of the Peruvian economy, which results in a proportion of males working away from home in the interior; with a higher standard of living in coastal cities many women prefer to remain there.

If the husband has a well-paid job his wife will not be expected to work but to supervise the running of the home and upbringing of the children. Peruvian men may practice a degree of misogyny but in middle-class homes the woman is in charge of the servants. This is certainly not the case lower down the social order, where women have to work extremely hard to maintain the home, look after the children and, quite probably, undertake some form of physically tiring employment to make ends meet.

Expletives Not Deleted . . .

Peruvians react quickly if they think they have been insulted. They will definitely say something and it will probably include a string of expletives. Peruvians rarely use expletives and the ones they do use would be considered mild by Western standards. They will mainly be directed at a man's mother (paradoxically reflecting the respect in which mothers are held) and it's possible that they will also be directed at his sexual prowess.

A Peruvian's pride may also mean that he, or she, is reluctant to seem ignorant or unknowing. Consequently, they will rarely say, "I don't know" ("*No sé*") when asked a question and will attempt to give an answer. It is usually best to compare the answers of two or three people when, for example, asking directions.

ATTITUDES TOWARD OTHERS

Peruvian society has a clear racial hierarchy with deep roots. This is rarely referred to and is not out in the open but it is all pervasive. Until independence (and after) the "white" elite kept themselves very much to themselves: racial segregation was enshrined in the class structure. Intermarriage was rare and any children of mixed blood (*mestizos*) resulting from affairs often went unrecognized. Many of the social rules applicable in Spain were followed in Lima. Women were not allowed to leave the house alone nor walk the streets without their *tapada* (equivalent to the Arab burka), which covered the whole head apart from one eye! The *tapada*, however, also provided women with a degree of freedom as the wearer was unrecognizable. Incognito she was able to visit public places, in contrast to many Peruvian women in the twentieth century. To view the goings-on in the street below, many colonial houses were built with screened balconies, some extremely ornate in the Moorish style, behind which women could sit. Some of the finest have been preserved and can be found in downtown Lima—Vargas Llosa wrote a play about them, *El loco de los balcones* (*The Madman of the Balconies*).

As in colonial times a colored skin is still associated with inferiority in Peru. Indigenous people, in the Andes and Amazon, and Black people are discriminated against. People with Andean features and *mestizos* are sometimes referred to by the derogatory term *cholo*. It was applied to the previous president, Alejandro Toledo, but as the lot of ordinary Peruvians improves, the term *cholo* is becoming acceptable as a unifying badge of identification among the masses.

Only in the mid-twentieth century did the *mestizo* class become the largest group in the population, within which the lighter the skin the greater the opportunity for social advancement. Consequently, to marry someone fairer than yourself is considered desirable. Peruvians to this day make assumptions about others based on their skin color. Membership in the elite creates employment opportunities and permits your children to attend private schools and universities.

Oriental migrants formed close-knit, mutually supportive communities and often developed specialist skills. Ultimately, they have achieved a slightly higher social standing. The Chinese were imported as indentured laborers to replace the Black slaves when they received their freedom (1854). They have gone on to become owners of corner stores, so there's a popular saying: "*Hay un chino en cada esquina*" (there's a Chinese on every street corner). The Japanese arrived either side of the Second World War as free immigrants to take advantage of commercial opportunities.

Peruvians, like most Latin Americans, are intensely patriotic. This reflects their hard-won independence and the manipulative nature of political rule over the last two centuries.

Wars with Ecuador and Chile have also shaped this mentality. Many ordinary Peruvians distrust Chileans, as to a lesser extent does the business community. Despite their Spanish blood, many Peruvians feel a lack of respect for Spain and the manner in which it ran Peru in colonial times. In certain circumstances Ecuadorians are referred to as *monos* (monkeys) while Bolivians are seen as the poor relations. Brazilians and Argentinians are well regarded.

THE NATIONAL ANTHEM

The Peruvian national anthem is internationally renowned as one of the least uplifting, with lines such as *"For a long time, the oppressed Peruvian dragged the ominous chain."* and *"Condemned to cruel servitude . . . he quietly whimpered."* For many years a major rewrite has been proposed, as standards of living improve, to boost morale and instill greater national pride.

While most foreign visitors will be readily welcomed throughout the country, Afro-Caribbeans may find that people are wary of them. This is mainly because there are relatively few Black people in Peru, especially away from the main cities and coastal towns south of Lima.

There is greater acceptance of gays and lesbians than just a decade ago. Many bars in the more fashionable areas of Lima openly welcome gay customers and in 2005 the first gay pride parade took place there. Discretion is still advisable, however, especially outside Lima.

Hey, Gringo!

"Hey, Gringo!" is quite a common call directed at any recognizable foreigner walking down the street, usually by children or young men. This is not an unfriendly sign, more a show of welcome and acknowledgment, perhaps that you have chosen to visit their neighborhood. The term originates from Mexico's war with the USA in the 1840s, when Mexicans shouted "Greens go (home)" at the US soldiers dressed in green uniforms—which transmuted into "gringo."

CUSTOMS &
TRADITIONS

THE CHURCH

The majority of customs and traditions in Peru
are inexorably linked to the Catholic Church.
Even at secular events and ceremonies there will
be a religious presence.

The link between the Church and Peru began
the day Pizarro landed and raised a cross on a
northern beach. His expedition had the full

blessing of the King of
Spain and the Pope, and
religious representatives
featured prominently at all
major events throughout
the Conquest. Though
gold and other treasures
may have been at the
forefront of the
conquistadores' minds,
conversion to Catholicism
was a strong secondary
aim and a major
justification for the
Conquest.

The indigenous belief system focused on the sun and other deities, and on the threats posed by numerous natural hazards. The Sun was the principal god, the Moon his wife, and their sons, the Inca rulers, their representatives on earth.

Catholic practices vary widely across modern Peru. In middle-class urban areas the Church is a bastion of tradition and the conservative Opus Dei movement has a significant presence. In many poorer urban areas a more liberal view of Catholic teachings has been adopted by those having to deal with severe poverty on a daily basis, while in the Andes many religious practices are intertwined with pre-Conquest beliefs.

FESTIVALS AND HOLIDAYS

As in other Latin American countries, fiestas feature prominently in Peruvian life—over 3,000 are held across the country throughout the year.

Each town has its own patron—a saint or the Virgin (*Virgen*)—and celebration of the patron is a major festival day each year. In some cases it has achieved a wider national significance and attracts visitors from outside the immediate area. The foundation day of the town can also be of great importance and an occasion for extensive festivities, especially in Lima (January 18) and Arequipa (August 15).

At times of major national holidays and the most important local *fiestas* transportation and accommodation are booked up several days in advance and prebooking is essential. On public holidays almost everything bar transportation, restaurants, and tourist-related services are closed. At *fiesta* times most services remain open but may have restricted hours.

THE FESTIVAL CALENDAR
January

Año Nuevo (New Year) is celebrated by a midnight mass, followed by a public holiday (January 1). It is an opportunity to party and set off fireworks. Don't be surprised to find small bonfires lining the streets—burning the old to welcome in the new. Another important tradition to bring good luck for the forthcoming year is for women to wear yellow underwear!

Bajada de Reyes (Epiphany, January 6) is a public holiday on which families meet up to mark the end of the festivities. On this day the Nativity is taken down, often accompanied by a party.

Concurso Nacional de Marinera (National Marinera Dance Contest, last two weeks of January) attracts hundreds of couples to Trujillo to compete. There are six age-based categories ranging from children under ten to the retired. The champions are held in very high regard.

THE MARINERA

Peru's national dance is a joyful, ritualistic display of flirtation and seduction in which the couple set out to provoke and enchant each other through precise choreography. The rhythm is supplied by guitars and a *cajón* (see page 110) or, in the north, a brass band. The Marinera has its origins on the north coast but has been influenced by

other dance forms, chiefly indigenous and Afro-Peruvian. It acquired its current name in 1879 when it was revised in honor of the naval hero Admiral Grau—"El Marinero." Over the years three different interpretations, distinctive in their costumes and music, have developed: Marinera Limeña (danced in Lima), Marinera Norteña (north coast, especially Trujillo), and Marinera Serrana (highlands). For La Norteña women wear a shawl and long skirt (in Lima it would be shorter), men wear trousers, a poncho, and a straw hat (in Lima they wear a suit), both dance barefoot (smart shoes in Lima), and both wave a white handkerchief throughout the dance.

February
Carnaval (Carnival) is an excuse for a month of celebrations beginning in early February and lasting until early March.

A Monthlong Party!

In some towns events are very much focused on a single week within the Carnaval period, but in others they continue for much of the month. It's a noisy, colorful event with a flavor all its own, especially in the Andes. On the street pedestrians need to keep their eyes open for water, flour, ink, and oil "bombs" flung from touring vehicles! Processions, fireworks, and concerts all feature, while for many it is just an excuse for a lengthy party. In processions revelers dress up in spectacular homemade costumes, which are often themed—groups wearing white, purple, and lilac dresses might represent the different colored flowers of the potato—and dance through the streets accompanied by bands. Cajamarca claims the biggest and best Carnival celebration.

Virgen de la Candelaria (February 1–7) is celebrated throughout the Andes but is especially important in Puno. Dance groups from all around Lake Titicaca converge there for the week: this is an excellent opportunity to take in traditional Andean music and dances such as the Huayno. The Virgen will be paraded around town accompanied by formally dressed officials and *campesinos* in masked animal costumes representing the spirits of pumas, condors, and llamas, among others.

Día Nacional de Pisco (Pisco National Day, February 8) is celebrated in towns that produce pisco (see page 105) along the coast south of Lima. A day to visit *bodegas* (wineries) to sample the finest piscos, accompanied by various local dishes such as *pallares* (butter bean casserole).

March/April

Festival de la Vendimia (Grape Harvest Festival, first weekend of March) occurs in towns south of Lima: Chincha, Lunahuana, and Ica. This is a great opportunity to visit not only large *bodegas* such as Tacama and Ocucaje, close to Ica, but also small, rustic, family-owned ones.

Semana Santa (Holy Week, or Easter) is a national vacation; Easter Thursday and Good Friday are public holidays. The long weekend allows many to get away, while for others it is a deeply religious festival. Ayacucho, in the central highlands, is the focus of celebratory fervor with many candlelit processions passing through the city, flower-petal paintings on the streets, and daily fairs. This city has the greatest density of churches of any in Peru but in most places the religious aspect of Holy Week is no longer as strong as it once was. As this is the last major holiday weekend of the summer nowadays the migration to the beaches is more notable than religious devotion.

El Señor de los Temblores ("Lord of the Earthquakes") is celebrated in some southern Andean towns, especially around Cuzco, on Easter Monday. This is a good example of the marriage of ancient rites with the established Church.

May

Día del Trabajo (Labor Day, May 1) is a public holiday—a day for relaxing.

Fiesta de la Cruz (Festival of the Cross, May 1) is commemorated in the southern highlands and on the coast with processions to the crosses positioned high on hills overlooking towns.

Día de la Madre (Mother's Day, second Sunday of May) is an important event given the significance of the mother within Peruvian society (see

Gender Roles, page 51). Most families take their mother to dine in a restaurant.

June

Inti Raymi (June 24), in Cuzco, marks the winter solstice. It is now one of the major national festivities attracting thousands of Peruvians and foreigners to a series of events throughout June culminating on June 24 in a procession from the Qoricancha palace, in the heart of Cuzco, up to the ramparts of Sacsahuaman. Several hundred citizens dress up in fine costumes as the Inca, his attendants, and pilgrims from the *suyos* (quarters of the Inca empire) to enact ceremonies that include a speech by the Inca, in Quechua, to the Sun (Inti) and those present. It is possible to stand atop the ruins to view the ceremonies from a distance, but the best view is from the stands (tickets must be bought in advance).

Día del Padre (Father's Day, third Sunday of June) is just as important as Mother's Day and is similarly celebrated.

San Pedro y San Pablo (Saints Peter and Paul, June 29) is celebrated on the coast as these are the patron saints of fishermen. Flotillas of fishing boats carry images of the saints out to sea for a "floating" service.

Qoyllur Rit' i (50–58 days after Easter Sunday) is celebrated in a remote high Andean valley at 15,400 ft. (4,700 m), close to Mount Ausangate (20,900 ft., 6,372 m), 95 miles (150 km) southeast of Cuzco. Once marking the reappearance of the Pleiades constellation, the festival was Christianized in 1780 after a shepherd boy had a vision of a white Christ child. The weeklong festivity is no longer a small local celebration but attracts thousands of people. The area's *campesinos* are still there singing, dancing, making offerings to the *apus* (mountain gods) and other spirits, and hacking ice from the glacier high above the valley to take home to prepare the ritual *chicha* beer, but they are now joined by a multitude of onlookers. The occasional death from exposure is seen as payment to Pachamama (Mother Earth) and a good omen. A church has been built in the valley, where regular services are held during the week.

July
Día de la Independencia or **Fiestas Patrias** (Independence Day, July 27 from midday, 28, and

29) is a national holiday. Homes are legally obliged to fly the national flag or risk a fine. Aside from those participating in lengthy parades, many Peruvians take the opportunity to go on vacation. Parades are dominated by civic dignitaries, with every military, educational, and health institution represented. The largest parade, attended by the president, is held in Avenida Brasil, Lima, and is dominated by military personnel and equipment; it is televised nationwide.

Yawar Fiesta (28 July), held in very traditional remoter communities in Apurimac, is another occasion in which the struggle between ancient traditions and more recent history is represented. The main event involves the tying of a captured condor, representing all that is Andean, to the back of a bull, representing all that came with the Spanish Conquest. The brief, bloody ritual sees the bull desperately try to shake off the condor, which, in turn, pecks away at the back of the bull. The condor is then released to fly off to the *apus* carrying the aspirations of the community.

August

Waman Raymi (second Sunday of August), held in Huamachuco, is a smaller, less sophisticated version of Inti Raymi. It is combined with festivities marking the founding of the town on August 15. At both events expect to see "*los turcos*"—*campesinos* from a local community whose menfolk dress up in multilayered skirts. Waman Raymi attracts few *gringos* so the

associated events are considerably less touristy
than at its Cuzco counterpart.

Santa Rosa de Lima (August 30) is the day
celebrating the patron saint of Peru and a public
holiday. It is principally celebrated by the military
with marches and parades.

September

Festival Internacional de la Primavera (Spring
Festival, last week of September) is an important
event on the coast, especially in Trujillo. There
are beauty pageants, processions, cultural events,
and horse (*caballos de paso*) shows.

October

Batalla de Angamos (Battle of Angamos,
October 8) commemorates Peru's only naval
victory (1879), against Chile in the War of the
Pacific, and is a public holiday.

El Señor de los Milagros (Lord of the Miracles,

last two weeks of October) is observed in Lima. Devotees wear purple for most of the month but the big processions only occur on October 18, 19, and 28, and November 1. It commemorates the miraculous survival of a painted image of Christ crucified, in the church of Las Nazarenas, in central Lima, in 1655, following an earthquake.

November

Todos los Santos (All Saints, November 1) is a public holiday.

Día de los Muertos (Day of the Dead, November 2) is important to all sectors of Peruvian society. For the coastal populace it's a day to visit the cemetery and leave flowers on the graves of ancestors. In the Andes the day links the Catholic rites of the previous day with traditional Inca practices related to the belief that ancestral spirits visit their relatives at this time of the year.

Puno Founding Day (November 5) is noteworthy because, aside from the events normally associated with a founding day, there is a reenactment of the arrival of Manco Capac and Mama Ocllo, the founders of the Inca dynasty (see page 25), by *tortora* (reed) raft from the lake. Dance and music groups congregate from surrounding villages and the entertainment spreads throughout the town.

December

Inmaculada Concepción (December 8) is a public holiday.

Nacimiento (Nativity, mid-December) involves the setting up of the most important "Christmas decoration" in a Peruvian home. It can occupy a sizeable portion of the living room, or garden— almost life-size figurines are not unknown!

At **Navidad** (Christmas, December 24–25) the tradition of going to midnight mass (*Misa del Gallo*) on Christmas Eve (*Noche Buena*) and eating afterward is declining: most people go to mass earlier in the evening. Christmas dinner is now normally eaten at 9–10:00 p.m.—roast chicken or turkey, according to income. Gifts are opened after midnight, traditionally accompanied by *panetone* (cake) and hot chocolate—if you have room!

SAINTS' DAYS AND PILGRIMAGES

Few Peruvians now celebrate saints' days, even if they bear a saint's name. Once their saint's day would have been celebrated like a second birthday, with gifts and a party.

Many Peruvians are sufficiently devout to attend mass on Sundays and during the week to enter a church when passing to say a quick prayer or seek divine comfort. The most committed take things a step further and make periodic pilgrimages to a major shrine, though there is no single shrine of national importance, such are the distances in Peru.

In the north devotees flock to Motupe,
55 miles (90 km) north of Chiclayo, on August 5,
to participate in the procession of the Cruz de
Chalpón (Cross of Chalpón) from a nearby
hillside cave through the village.

In the south the Fiesta de la Virgen de Chapí
(Virgin of Purification) draws pilgrims in their
thousands from nearby Arequipa, on May 1, to
the Sanctuario de Chapi (Sanctuary of Chapi).
The huge line of vehicles stretched out across the
desert en route to the Sanctuary is a sight to
behold, while other worshipers take about fifteen
hours to walk there from Arequipa—at night, to
avoid the heat.

Near Lima pilgrims visit Santa Rosa de Quives,
the retreat of the patron saint of Peru, 25 miles
(40 km) north of Lima. The main event is on
August 30 but visitors come to view her home
and the Sanctuary throughout the year.

In the first week of October, El Señor de Luren,
in Ica, also attracts pilgrims to all-night
processions through the city.

SHAMANISM AND OTHER TRADITIONS

The lives of many Peruvians involve or are
governed by a synthesis of traditions or
something stronger, but few would openly refer
to them as superstitions. In many Andean
communities non-Christian rituals are likely to
be far more significant on a daily basis than the
power of the Church, though most people follow

both traditions. In the Amazon region the Catholic Church plays a minor role among indigenous people: nowadays Evangelical groups often have a greater presence.

In the Andes there are many firmly believed myths such as, in the Cuzco area, that of the Ukukus (immortal bear-men who bring fertility) and the Kukuchis (invisible cannibal spirits who roam the glaciers). During fiestas, *campesinos* may dress as these beings or as animal spirits.

Andean Myths

In the remoter Andes the myth of the *pishtaco* still prevails. Parents tell their young children that they must never stray too far or they will be grabbed by the *pishtaco*, a tall, blond, bearded giant who needs to consume human fat. It is still possible for some travelers (*gringos*)— depending on their appearance—to find children cowering or running away from them in fear. The idea of the *pishtaco* may well have originated in colonial times, reflecting the cruelty of Spanish rule. It was revived more recently when there was a spate of kidnappings associated with forced organ donations.

Most people's involvement with indigenous traditions is through healing rituals and herbal medicine. In most markets, especially in Andean towns, there is a section known as the *mercado de los brujos* (witches' market). The stalls display a variety of herbs, seeds, spices, dried animal parts, and exotic trinkets for use by healers. This section of the main market (*mercado central*) in Chiclayo, actually a coastal city, is one of the most comprehensive in South America.

In a traditional southern Andean home the dried fetus of a llama will be buried in the foundations to ensure the longevity of the house; the cadaver of a crow is suspended over the marital bed to bring fertility to the couple, and a piece of aloe vera is nailed over the front entrance for good health and to ward off evil spirits.

Curanderos (healers) practice all over Peru. They will usually use a combination of herbs, plants, effigies, seeds, and charms to treat patients for anything from ill health to marital discord. Their "gifts" are considered to be hereditary and generation after generation may follow the same path. One of the more unusual approaches involves the use of a guinea pig (*cuy*). The *curandero* passes the live *cuy* over the naked torso of the patient. The animal is then killed and cut open, whereupon the healer undertakes a diagnosis of the patient from the color and condition of its intestines.

A more common ritual in which visitors may find themselves participating is the making of offerings (*pagos*). *Pagos* usually consist of a symbolic offering to Pachamama and all that she can provide or to the *apus* to ward off natural disasters. For a *curandero* this may involve a lengthy ceremony incorporating coca leaves, seeds, feathers, and *chicha* beer. For most people, including the visitor, it requires that, prior to the consumption of a drink, a little is first poured onto the ground.

The Shamanic Tradition

In recent years there has been a reassessment and reemergence of indigenous knowledge, customs, and language. This includes the revitalization of shamanic practices, and consequently many indigenous Andean and Amazonian communities now adhere more confidently to the shamanic traditions of their ancestors. Traditional shamans, however, who serve as a combination of doctor, priest, and healer, are found in a declining number of communities as Western influences impact upon the younger generation. The surviving shamans tend to be elderly while younger healers, with lesser knowledge and powers, tend to be referred to as *curanderos*.

Traditional Andean and Amazonian communities believe in the interconnectedness of the spirit and material worlds. Spirits are omnipresent and the shaman is their link and conduit. On a practical basis this means that most indigenous people find it hard to adjust to a structured, preplanned Western lifestyle. They are more likely to determine their day by observing the clouds and checking river levels, or listening for good or bad omens in the calls of particular animals and in events within their dreams. This is not something with which the casual visitor can immediately become fully familiar. It may take many months, if not years, to be accepted into an indigenous community and discover the intricate relationships that exist with the spiritual world.

In parts of western Amazonia a hallucinogenic vine, *ayahuasca*, plays an important role in the work of the shaman. A strong purgative, it should only be consumed according to a fixed procedure of dieting and abstaining from sexual activity in the preceding and subsequent days.

Interest in shamanic culture has also led to a growth in so-called "shamanic" tourism. One of the principal attractions for the participants is the taking of *ayahuasca*, but many true shamans are not prepared to indulge Western visitors.

The most important place for *curanderos* is Las Guaringas, in the northern Andes, northeast of Piura. Many healers have gathered together to attend to the afflicted, who arrive from all over the country. The nighttime ceremony will almost certainly involve drinking the juice of the foul-tasting, hallucinogenic San Pedro cactus, chanting, and dancing. The ritual ends with immersion in the freezing waters of a lake.

chapter four

MAKING FRIENDS

PART OF THE FAMILY

Peruvians like to have many friends and make them easily. Background and political ideology are two of the most important factors in a friendship. Close friends are expected to show loyalty, share important moments, enjoy life together, and support each other in times of need. In Peru a close friendship signifies more than a relationship between just two people—it is essential, especially for women, to become part of your friend's family and to treat them as if they were your own. On this basis you can drop in on a friend, or their family, at any time. An established friendship is seen as being for the long term and absence—abroad, for example—will not greatly affect it.

The metropolitan, educated Peruvian is open, friendly, and sociable. Peruvians from more humble rural backgrounds, however, are likely to be much more timid and reserved, history having taught them to be wary of strangers. The civil war years created a lot of suspicion amongst all echelons of society but most people now feel more trusting of others. You will find most Peruvians will be interested in meeting and talking to you.

Peruvians socialize with friends and colleagues outside the home, especially in cafés. After work it is common to meet up for *lonche* (see page 104) before going home. In summer groups of friends often head off to the beach, if they live near the coast, while in coastal towns the *malecón* (seafront) is a popular place for all age groups to stroll and chat. Similarly, the Plaza de Armas (main square), and smaller squares, in any town or city, is where people congregate to talk, eat ice cream, or have their photo taken. Don't be surprised if you are approached by locals wanting to know something about you or students with questions they hope you can answer.

If a Peruvian in your home country provides you with the contact details of a friend or family member, then expect to be received by them as a friend. They will go out of their way to ensure that you have everything you want, will assist you with your arrangements as best they can, and check that your plans seem sensible. You will probably also meet their family and friends.

If your language skills are not strong there are a couple of ways in which you can quickly win acceptance with Peruvians. They enjoy playing cards, so the ability to play Ocho Locos (Crazy Eights) or Casino while waiting for a bus, during a railway journey, or on a boat trip across Lake Titicaca, will make you popular. Also, they love to play football and will invite you to join in if you express the slightest interest. Many of them learn on small concrete playing fields, with five or six players a side (*fulbito*), which requires a high degree of skill—be warned! Larger earth fields are found in the Andes and the jungle. On the Uros islands, Lake Titicaca, you might be lucky enough to get a game on a "floating" reed playing pitch.

WHAT SHOULD I TALK ABOUT?
Peruvians are interested in a wide range of topics but initial questions are likely to revolve around where you are from, your family and profession, where you have been in Peru, and Peruvian food. It is a good idea to carry a few photos of your family, your home, and local neighborhood to stimulate the conversation. Few topics are really off-limits and quite quickly you can find yourself talking about music, films, politics, and football. Most Peruvian businessmen will be knowledgeable about English football—they may watch it most weekends—and older ones may well have a strong nostalgic interest in Western rock music from the 1970s–80s. It is unlikely, however, that the conversation will swing round to the weather or, at the other end of the spectrum, very personal matters.

Topics that should be avoided at all times are those related to illness, sex, and money. Remarks with a sexual connotation that might seem quite innocent to Westerners are taboo in mixed company in Peru. If asked to express an opinion about something of a sexual nature, most Peruvians will laugh it off or make a bland comment to avoid embarrassment. Only among a group of close men friends might it be possible to be more risqué. Discussions of financial matters should be kept general: nothing personal, such as the value of your home or the size of your salary.

Peruvians are often interested in the cost of flying to Peru and comparative prices of various goods. Sometimes it may be tactful, because of the income difference, to understate certain costs—use your judgment. Taxi drivers are a good source of information, especially in Lima; many are professionals supplementing a meager income. One topic that Peruvians will be happy to talk about endlessly is food, regional variations and where you have eaten.

PERUVIAN HOSPITALITY

Peruvians take pride in offering hospitality. Once a friendship begins you can expect to be invited out for drinks, or a meal in a restaurant, or to a place that you have expressed an interest in visiting. This would always be with colleagues or their friends, never alone—Peruvians like to enjoy themselves in groups. Dress casually but err on the smart side. You won't be expected to contribute and there's no need to feel obliged to issue the next invitation: you are in Peru and you will be looked after without compromise (*sin compromiso*). If your friendship blossoms then a first invitation will shortly be followed by another. The idea behind this is that if your friend has the opportunity to visit your country (even if this is extremely unlikely) then he will hope to receive similar reciprocal treatment.

As a friendship becomes more established you might be invited back to their home for a meal, again with a group of colleagues or friends. Guests are not expected to do anything but to receive and appreciate their host's hospitality. A gift is not usually expected either.

TIMEKEEPING

Peruvians, like most South Americans, are not great timekeepers, but things are improving. If you need to be somewhere on time you will be advised that it is *hora inglesa/en punto* (English time/on time); otherwise, like them, you can follow *hora peruana*, but they will expect you to be more punctual. This allows you to be up to half an hour late. An hour is within the bounds of acceptability, but two hours may be pushing it. A quick call on a cell phone should be made if you are likely to be over an hour late.

Peruvians aren't only late arrivers, they are also slow leavers, lingering over a departure. It can easily take an hour to down the last drink, finish a conversation (there is always more to discuss), and say good-bye. On this basis it is a good idea to announce that you need to leave well in advance.

You will need to arrive on time for a visit to the theater or cinema, even if the show starts a few minutes later than programed—probably due to the late arrival of much of the audience! However, it is worth noting that flight, bus, and train departures are no longer a law unto themselves and, in general, do depart at the appointed time and require you to arrive some time beforehand.

The Two Hour Advance Invite!

The best timekeeping is reserved for occasions such as a baptism (*bautismo*), wedding (*boda*), and funeral (*funeral*). Invitations may specify arriving up to two hours prior to the event, to ensure that everyone is there on time. However, this won't prevent many guests from arriving in a mad rush in the last five minutes!

NEIGHBORS

In middle-class suburbs people live either in impersonal apartment blocks or in well-protected houses and usually leave them by car. Most people know who their neighbors are but encounters with them are infrequent. If there is a chance meeting on the stairs, or in the lobby, however, people will stop to chat. Many apartment blocks have a small committee to deal with maintenance matters and this is another means by which you may meet your neighbors on a regular basis. In more luxurious blocks the *portero* (concierge) or *cuidante* (caretaker) is the link between everyone and the local neighborhood. As neighbors are neither family nor work colleagues, it is unlikely that they will become part of your social circle.

In more tightly packed areas noise is the principal source of conflict between neighbors. The concept of social responsibility is not well developed so be prepared for your neighbors, from time to time, to play music at high volume at various hours of the day and night.

EXPATRIATE ASSOCIATIONS

Most expatriate communities in Peru are small and there are only a handful of associations or clubs per community, if that. Your embassy will have a list of them. For British visitors the Peruvian-British Cultural Association provides a good library and occasional cultural events, and can facilitate contact with other long-term British residents. The North American equivalent is the ICPNA (Instituto Cultural Peruano-Norte Americano), which is increasing its presence across Peru. Both offer language classes and an opportunity to meet local people interested in the English-speaking worlds.

For those planning to travel widely within the country a useful group is the South American Explorers Club (www.saexplorers.org).

SPORTS AND OTHER CLUBS

The best sports facilities are offered by private membership clubs. You may need a sponsor to join. These usually offer a gym, tennis, racquetball, squash, and swimming depending on the size and location of the club. In Lima there are two extremely exclusive golf clubs.

Most towns and cities now contain modern gyms with a range of exercise equipment. Temporary membership is usually available.

On the outskirts of most large towns and cities there are recreational clubs (*recreos*). At the lower end of the range they are small, rustic establishments with a football-cum-volleyball playing field and a restaurant, though you can also bring your own food. At the top end they are members-only and consist of an attractive enclosed area of landscaped countryside with good sporting facilities, barbeques, restaurants, and chalets (in case you wish to overnight).

chapter five

THE PERUVIANS AT HOME

PERUVIAN HOMES

A home, whether in an urban or a rural area, will of course reflect its owner's economic status. The traditional architecture and building materials may vary according to region. The Amazon region, for example, is warm and wet all year-round so houses are often built on stilts and are quite open to the elements. In the Andes *adobe* (mud) bricks are the main building material, walls are thick and windows small to protect against extremes of heat in the day and cold at night. The coastal desert is very hot for much of the year so houses are traditionally built from *adobe* and bamboo.

Modern materials, bricks and concrete, are increasingly used in all regions.

In cities there is a sharp division between wealthier and poorer areas. In the former people live in substantial villas or modern apartment complexes, sometimes incorporating spectacular design features: swimming pools on the top of twenty-story blocks are not unknown. In these districts residents may still employ guards (a common feature in the civil war years of the 1980s and 1990s) to patrol and check vehicles. ID may still need to be shown to enter the most exclusive districts unless one is accompanied.

In middle-class areas people live in small brick houses that commonly appear half-built as additional rooms or floors are added later according to finances and, frequently, to provide a home for a child on marrying. Houses are designed so that they are inward looking, with small patios, rather than having many external windows, letting light in. A living room or large kitchen is used on a daily basis, while a smarter sitting room is used for guests and on more formal family occasions. Many Peruvians feel more comfortable retiring to bed to watch television in the evening rather than using the sitting room. In the kitchen cooking is by gas, from a cylinder, as few can afford electric stoves. Most houses have a small garden but this is primarily for aesthetic reasons and not for the children to play in. Cars are parked in a garage or inside security gates, and there is generally some form of security to deter intruders on external walls, including electric fences. Garbage is collected daily from the front of each house.

On the periphery of the cities live the poor, often rural migrants, in shantytown settlements. These are known as *pueblos jovenes* (young towns) and comprise about half the area and inhabitants of most cities. They have high crime rates and are best avoided by visitors. Many of the constructions seem flimsy, being built initially from reed matting, sacking, plastic, and wood. It is estimated that the value of home improvements in the shantytowns runs to several million US dollars a year but this is not always obvious to the traveler looking out of a bus window.

Since the 1960s Peru's urban areas have been transformed. The 1970 earthquake displaced thousands to Chimbote and Lima, both of which, along with most other cities, then took thousands more migrants resulting from the civil war in the 1980s. Lima's population rose spectacularly, from three million in 1970 to eight million by 2000. As a result Peru's urban areas, where 78 percent of the population now live, have changed out of all recognition. Given the desert environment and a lack of resources, it has been a challenge to improve the infrastructure and provide adequate services. Occasional water shortages and electricity outages occur in most cities.

Home Help

Many families in Peru—almost without exception among the wealthy—employ a woman (*muchacha*) to help run the house. In most cases she does the shopping, cooking, cleaning, washing, and ironing. Traditionally, she lived within the family home, though since the social upheavals of the 1980s and 1990s many now come in on a daily basis. Other full- or part-time employees may include nannies and gardeners.

How they are treated varies considerably. In some families the relationship is informal, with a nanny playing a major role in the upbringing of the children and accompanying the family on vacation. Many remain for years with the same family and become a trusted family member. In others, however, the *muchacha* is required to wear a uniform, and is treated much more as a servant.

These services are not seen as excessive: on the contrary, they are considered necessary by most people with at least a modest income.

DAILY LIFE

Basic survival is the major daily concern for the majority of Peruvians. Most find themselves having to work incredibly hard, leaving home before 6:00 a.m. to start their working day. The poorest sectors of society may have a three-hour commute each day—in from their shantytown on an old cramped bus, then working in a heavily polluted roadside shop or market.

The average urban middle-class worker begins his day early at 6–7:00 a.m. Breakfast at home is often rushed because of the time needed to commute. For office staff, the working day begins around 8:30 a.m., and a break is not usually taken before lunch. Lunch starts at 12:00 and lasts until 2:00 p.m. for most workers, much earlier than in some Latin countries. It is usually a fairly quick affair, a *menú* (see page 103) in a local restaurant; few people go home for lunch nowadays.

In offices the working day ends at 5:30–6:00 p.m., though shops stay open until 7–8:00 p.m. A light evening meal (*lonche*) is eaten as soon as workers arrive home at around 7:00 p.m.

Shopping

Most families shop almost daily in local markets for their basic needs though supermarkets are increasingly used in urban areas. This is supplemented by purchases from street vendors, who tour neighborhoods with their carts offering bread, fruit, or vegetables and announce their arrival by blowing a horn or ringing a bell. Buying food daily ensures that it is always fresh and hygiene levels are maintained. Few Peruvians would dream of eating the previous day's bread for breakfast.

Unfortunately much of the best produce is now exported, or only available in supermarkets. A visit to the local shops or market is very much a social occasion, an opportunity to chat and gossip with vendors and neighbors. In Peru shopping, like business (see page 142), is all about personal relationships, underpinned by the idea that you will get a better deal in terms of price and quality by developing a strong personal contact with a vendor (*casero*). This mutually beneficial relationship of trust is very important for most Peruvians.

Supermarkets have now spread to all the larger cities, though the greatest concentration remains in Lima. They are usually attached to smart commercial centers, which include cinemas and boutique-style shops. The market leaders are Metro, Wong, and Tottus, all Chilean owned, and Plaza Vea, Peruvian owned. They all offer a wide range of fresh produce that can be relied upon to be of high quality. A variety of promotional samples means that you can always taste before you buy.

Money Exchange

The Nuevo Sol has been very stable against the US dollar for several years. Peruvians are increasingly trusting of their currency, which they use for most day-to-day transactions. Etched into the memory of most adults is the high inflation of the late 1980s (100 percent a day at one point), in which many lost their entire savings. Consequently, wealthier Peruvians keep most of their savings in US dollars and some have accounts abroad. Major purchases are often made in US dollars. If needed, they will buy dollars through a licensed *cambista* (money changer, often the same one each time for the reasons given above), who waits each day on a designated street corner to catch passing trade.

LEISURE TIME

Peruvians spend a large proportion of their leisure time with their family. The family is at the heart of Peruvian life and on weekends they meet up with other family members and friends for excursions to the beach, a restaurant, or *recreos*. After an extended lunch a popular game is Sapo, in which players throw coins at slots in the top of a box; the value of each slot varies but the highest score is gained by throwing the coin into the mouth of the *sapo* (a small bronze frog)—it's not as hard as it sounds!

The beach is a major attraction, but care needs to be taken with tides and currents (check with the locals) and facilities are often limited. In the summer months thousands of Limeños leave the city for the beaches to the south, where they may have a chalet, or they camp.

CHILDREN

In the wealthiest families children may be brought up by a nanny but there is still strong parental involvement. In poorer families, parents may well have to spend lengthy periods working away from home, so older children help to bring up younger siblings and to supplement the family income.

In richer, urban families children receive decent schooling, usually in private institutions, and will

not be expected to assist at home. Vacations are
spent out of the city at a beach house; there is no
question of their looking for a temp job. Children
from very wealthy families make frequent trips to
the USA to shop and relax. Many of them will rarely
leave their immediate suburb in Lima, other than to
fly to Florida and, increasingly, the Caribbean,
Chile, and Argentina.

Parents are quite intrusive in their children's
relationships. They will expect to be introduced to
a prospective partner at an early stage, far sooner
than in a Western relationship. Parental approval for
a partner is extremely important and it will quickly
be made known if the choice is thought unsuitable
due to background or ethnicity. Most parents will
expect their children to "marry up" to improve
their social and career prospects.

In stark contrast, in some urban areas, especially
Lima, "street children" can be seen sleeping rough
in parks, or on sidewalks.

Family Events

At all social levels, the extended family gathers regularly to celebrate family events and public holidays, as well as meeting most weekends in smaller numbers.

At important family gatherings and official occasions children will be expected to look their best and behave immaculately. Girls wear a pretty dress and smart shoes, and decorate their hair, though the latest fashions are increasingly being worn. Boys wear a suit and tie for most festivities.

Birthdays are celebrated with a big party, usually at home, to which the extended family is invited. Cards are not sent but presents are given.

For girls the big party marking their passage to adulthood is held at fifteen years of age and is known as Quinceañero. They will wear a white dress and host an evening party for family and friends. There is no such occasion for boys.

EDUCATION

Education is important to Peruvians. Primary school enrollment is high even in the shantytowns and rural areas, where pupils may have to walk long distances to their rudimentary school. The academic year runs from March to December, with major vacations mid-December to early March and two weeks in August.

Preschooling is common in the cities but not in rural areas. Local kindergartens (*jardins*) take three- to five-year-olds for a morning session for a small fee.

Many of the best schools are run by Catholic orders and parents must be married to have any chance of their child gaining a place there.

Primary Schools

Children begin compulsory schooling at six years old. There are six grades of primary (*primaria*) school (up to eleven years). Most schools are state run and follow a core national curriculum set by the Ministry of Education. Class sizes frequently exceed forty pupils and may contain as many as sixty where several year groups are taught together. Private schools not only offer better facilities but much smaller classes and a wider curriculum. English is taught in private schools and many state schools, while Quechua is taught in remoter Andean schools. The school day runs from 8:00 a.m. to 1:00 p.m., and there may also be classes on Saturday mornings. All state school children wear a uniform consisting of gray trousers or skirt, white shirt, and gray jumper.

Secondary Schools

Secondary (*secundaria*) school is compulsory up to the age of sixteen but many pupils drop out without completing their studies. For those wishing to do well the system is highly competitive and requires students to undertake additional studies outside school. By Western standards the curriculum would be regarded as highly traditional, rooted in nationalism and traditional "chalk and talk" teaching methods; this reflects the lack of resources and facilities. With respect to the emphasis placed on philosophy and logic, however, older students may well get a better deal than their US counterparts.

During their schooling, especially at secondary level, students are expected to participate in a series of events several times a year. The Independence Day celebrations, for example, involve marching and parading, often in extreme heat, for several hours.

In the last few years an increasing feature of secondary school life has been the end of school trip (*viaje de promoción*), in addition to the final party (*fiesta de promoción*). For students in poorer districts this may consist of a two-day coach trip to a nearby resort, while wealthier pupils may fly for a weeklong visit to Cuzco or Arequipa. The end of secondary schooling is marked by a formal graduation ceremony; these are also, increasingly, being held at the end of primary and even kindergarten education.

University

On completing their school studies most students immediately embark upon two months of revision for the university exams in March. Students from richer families may attend a special academy to prepare themselves for these. The successful students start university in April, while those who have not passed return to the academies before retaking the exams a few months later.

The university system is divided into national (state) and private universities. The former charge minimal fees; the latter have grown greatly in number over the last decade but charge higher fees. The fees charged to students by private universities depend on family income and the type of school attended: the better the school the higher the fees. Students also need family members willing to provide accommodation and cover their basic living needs for the duration of their studies. As with the schooling system almost all the top universities are in Lima.

LEARNING ENGLISH

Learning English is an important additional skill, seen as a way of increasing life chances. With Peru's economy firmly within the US sphere, and international tourism of such importance, a reasonable grasp of English is essential for most professionals. However, French and German influences are also strong and many young professionals may speak three languages.

In remoter areas people will only speak a smattering of English, while the first language of many women or older people will be their indigenous tongue. Many towns have English academies offering courses to supplement the school curriculum.

THE MEDIA
TV and Radio

Television is the most popular form of home entertainment—witness the multitude of aerials rising up from the shantytowns. There are seven main television channels, only one of which is state run: Channel 7 (Canal 7). Canal 56 broadcasts all Congressional proceedings and government statements. During Fujimori's time in the 1990s private channels came under heavy pressure to toe the government line, but have since reasserted their independence. Several can be received across most of the country, apart from very remote rural areas, which rely on DVDs. Many wealthier Peruvians and all but the cheapest hotels in accessible areas subscribe to cable television, which means CNN and BBC news channels are received across much of the country.

Telenovelas (soap operas) commence mid-morning and can be watched all day. Most originate from elsewhere in Latin America, notably Venezuela, Mexico, and Brazil (dubbed from Portuguese). Interminable, formulaic, often poorly acted, and with improbable plot lines, they provide a distraction from the harsher realities of life. Peru's own soaps are different. Recently several historical costume dramas with an eye for detail and significantly more watchable than their foreign counterparts have been very popular.

Television game shows are popular but often involve the humiliation of the contestants, who are attempting to win a relatively small prize but one that could make a significant difference to their lives. Other successes include the Peruvian equivalent of *American Idol* or *Pop Idol*, sports programs (especially football), and the news. There are also occasional high-quality Peruvian wildlife and historical programs.

Radio comes into its own in the Andes and the jungle, as the way that many communities maintain contact with the outside world in the absence of television and newspapers. The best radio stations for news are Radioprogramas del Peru and Cadena Peruana de Noticias.

The Press
Newspapers are widely available only in the major cities: the main national papers such as *El Comercio* and *La República*, plus local publications. *El Comercio* is a quality broadsheet consisting of several sections not unlike *The Times/New York Times*, with good international news coverage. *La República* is a serious tabloid format paper with a liberal-left approach. There are several lowbrow tabloids featuring even less news than their UK counterparts. *Caretas* is an informative, right-leaning, weekly current affairs magazine similar to *Time* magazine or *The Spectator*. A separate insert, *Ellos y Ellas*, focuses on Peruvian social gossip.

TIME OUT

FOOD

Peruvian food has a variety and inventiveness that make it one of the great cuisines of the world. It is, in fact, many cuisines, reflecting the rich diversity of traditional regional produce. Peruvians are passionate about their cuisine, which is now being brought to international prominence by chefs such as Gaston Acurio.

Along the coast *comida criolla* and seafood (*mariscos*) are favorites; in the Andes potato and maize (corn) provide the staple for an array of meat dishes; and in the Amazon fish is the principal ingredient. Supplementing these regional dishes is a range of exotic fruits and vegetables, many rarely seen outside Peru. And, especially on the coast, your meal isn't complete without a good dollop of fiery *ají* (chili sauce).

Ceviche—the National Dish

A legacy of Japanese migration to Peru, *ceviche* is far removed from its sushi origins but equally delicious. Usually, *ceviche* consists of flakes of firm white fish marinated in lime juice with plenty of chopped red onion and *ají*. It is served with boiled potatoes, including sweet potato, and a chunk of maize. *Ceviche* must only be consumed freshly prepared and, therefore, should not be eaten in the Andes. However, *ceviche de trucha* (trout) is an extremely tasty Andean alternative.

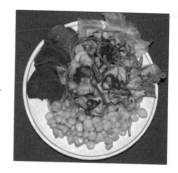

Comida Criolla

Comida criolla integrates ancient pre-Columbian foods and Spanish cuisine. It's also commonly associated today with the cuisine of Peru's small Black population. Their culinary influence has spread disproportionately through coastal cuisine: many Afro-Peruvians are employed as cooks.

Dishes include *tamales* (made from processed maize mash) and *humitas* (made from sweetcorn mash), stuffed with pieces of meat, egg, olives, and onion, wrapped in a banana or maize leaf, and boiled. They are served for breakfast and as a tasty starter. Other popular dishes include *cau-cau*: slivers of tripe cooked with diced potato and spices; and *tacu-tacu*: refried beans and rice with pieces of fish or meat added.

Rice

Despite Peru's having given the potato to the world, it is rice that has become the ubiquitous component of most Peruvian meals. Even if you insist quite vehemently that you want potato, you will still get rice as well! In the Andes potato is used more widely, as are other traditional crops such as the highly nutritious grains *quinoa* and *kiwicha*, both often used in soups.

Potatoes

Potatoes were unknown beyond the Andes until the Spanish rode up into the mountains and, subsequently, introduced the tuber to Europe.

Over 800 varieties grow in Peru, ranging from the bright yellow with a floury consistency, to the

small *chuños*, which are soaked immediately upon harvest in the freezing water of a mountain stream. They are then dried beneath the high altitude sun ready for winter storage. Most commonly used in soups, they are usually gray in color and firm in texture, while their flour is brilliant white.

In a big market the potato dealers occupy a large area selling upward of twenty varieties. Peruvians insist that only a certain type of potato should be used in a particular dish.

Cuy

No visit to the Andes is complete for the carnivore without tucking into low-cholesterol alpaca steak and *cuy* (guinea pig). Served fried, roasted, or stuffed, a half *cuy* is a fair meal if you can stomach the fact that it is likely to be served with head and feet intact.

Breakfast, Lunch, and Dinner

Breakfast (*desayuno*) is eaten early in rural areas and is often a substantial meal consisting of a thick soup, fried egg with rice, or fried fish. A more typical "continental" breakfast is consumed in urban areas but may include *tamales* and *chicharrones* (pieces of fried pork).

A common mid-morning snack on the coast is *churros*, a sweet pancake filled with *manjarblanco* (cinnamon-spiced liquid fudge, or *dulce de leche*).

Lunch (*almuerzo*) is served from midday and is often the main meal of the day. The best option is a set three-course *menú* offering a soup or salad, a choice of main dishes, a dessert, and a drink. This comes in two forms—*Económico*, the simpler and cheaper, and *Ejecutivo*, offering more elaborate dishes and bigger portions, but still good value.

Dinner (*cena*) is often only eaten out. Many Peruvians eat a lighter evening meal (*lonche*), which commonly includes *pollos a la brasa*.

Desserts

The enormous diversity of tropical fruits—including custard apple (*chirimoya*), mango, *lucuma*, papaya, and pineapple—produces some truly delicious pies, mousses, and ice creams.

MORE PERUVIAN SPECIALTIES

- *Anticuchos*: barbecued beef-heart "kebabs."
- *Ají de gallina*: shredded chicken stew with grated pecan nuts.
- *Pollo a la brasa*: the Peruvian version of grilled chicken; when it's good you will never want to eat at KFC again!
- *Seco de cordero/cabrito*: lamb or goat stewed with *chicha* (maize beer) and coriander.
- *Papa a la Huancaina*: potatoes served with a spicy cheese sauce—a popular starter.
- *Papa rellena*: deep-fried mashed potato stuffed with vegetables, olives, egg (and meat)—often sold by street vendors.
- *Causa*: layers of mashed potato, with combinations of avocado, chicken, tuna, or prawns mixed with mayonnaise, in between.
- *Empanadas*: small pastries stuffed with vegetables and meat or chicken, commonly served as a snack.

DRINKS

The range of beverages includes some distinctive offerings. Peru has its very own fizzy drink (*gaseosa*) called Inca Cola, which stimulates a unique form of patriotism—there was a huge outcry when Coca-Cola bought into the company. Made from lemongrass and bright yellow in color, its taste has been likened to banana and to bubble gum. The essential accompaniment to Chinese food (*chifa*), it is widely consumed with other meals, especially *pollo a la brasa*.

The area under vine in Peru is not large but Tacama and Ocucaje wines are, generally, very drinkable. Chilean and Argentinian wines are more highly rated and likely to dominate lists in better restaurants. However, it is the clear brandy *pisco*—most refreshingly consumed in the *pisco sour* cocktail—for which grape production is most valued.

PISCO SOUR

(TO SERVE FIVE PEOPLE)

3 units of *pisco* (the less smooth
pisco puro variety)
1 unit of lime juice (never lemon)
1 unit of sugar predissolved in a little
warm water and cooled
A couple of tumblers of crushed ice
1 egg white (optional)

Mix all together in a blender; adjust quantities to suit taste. Serve with a dusting of cinnamon, if egg white is used to enhance the appearance.

The best *piscos* are drunk neat (*Pisco Italia* or *Pisco Quebranta*, among others, and the blended, refined aromatic *pisco acholado*) and are revered like a good malt whiskey by a *pisquero*, a *pisco* connoisseur. The non-aromatic *Pisco puro* is usually used to make *pisco sour* and there are many other delicious cocktails such as *maracuya sour* and *coca sour*.

Peruvian breweries (there is one in all the main cities) were first established by German migrants. Cristal, brewed in Lima, and Cusqueña (Cuzco), are considered to be the smoothest and most drinkable.

The traditional maize beer, *chicha*, is made throughout the Andes. There are alcoholic and

nonalcoholic varieties, both a creamy yellow in color. The former, though initially refreshing after a trek, is an acquired taste in any quantity. Its availability can be determined by a red flag (often now a red plastic bag on the end of a pole) outside houses. The nonalcoholic *chicha morada*, made from purple maize, is dark purple in color.

Herbal teas are widely available but, sadly, a decent cup of coffee is almost impossible to find: most good coffee is exported. In many cafés, even in coffee-growing areas, only Nescafé or *café pasado* (liquid "coffee" essence, which you add to a cup of hot water) is available. English-style tea is, generally, an insipid tea bag. Milk is usually either evaporated or condensed.

EATING OUT

Eating is a favourite Peruvian pastime and, consequently, a common topic for conversation. A Peruvian will remember for years a small restaurant where he once ate a fine *cuy frito* (fried guinea pig) or delicious *tacu-tacu*. There are some superb restaurants, especially in Lima, which rank among the world's best. They are affordable and should not be missed.

There is some specialization among restaurants: the best *ceviche* is likely to be found in a *cevicheria*, for example, while others specialize in *comida criolla* or seafood (*mariscos*).

On weekends eating out is a great ritual for huge family parties, which occupy several tables in a restaurant for much of the afternoon. During the week it's more functional as workers take a quick bite in local family-run restaurants—no packed lunches here! Cafés offer lighter meals and snacks, and come into their own in the late afternoon and evenings.

Manual workers are often brought their lunch by a family member in a pyramid of pots to be eaten at their workplace, or they frequent market stalls. The latter may attract the more adventurous traveler but it's wise to check the level of cleanliness and always ensure the food is served freshly cooked and very hot.

Apart from Lima, where there is an extensive range of international cuisine, only Chinese food (*chifa*) is commonly found elsewhere, plus Italian food in major tourist and trekking centers. *Chifas* are sometimes the best option in smaller towns. Avoid fast-food chains, though Peru's own version of McDonald's—Bembo's—is worth a try.

TIPPING

There isn't a culture of tipping in Peru. In most restaurants and cafés you are not expected to tip, though in some upmarket restaurants customers may leave 10 percent. However, hotel porters at better hotels will expect a small tip to supplement their pay. Car drivers should be prepared to give something to the watchman who keeps an eye on their car when parked in the street outside a restaurant or shop—up to $1. It's more a payment than a tip. Taxi drivers do not expect to be paid more than the prenegotiated fare.

NIGHTLIFE AND PEÑAS

Music and dance are essential ingredients in the lives of most Peruvians. Almost everyone, however humble their background, grows up knowing how to play a musical instrument and to dance. This, combined with their love of food, means that Peruvians know how to have a good time when they go out.

There are few bars outside the major cities and jungle towns, and even there they may be attached to a smarter restaurant or hotel. Only in the upmarket Lima suburbs of Miraflores and Barranco are there individualistic bars ranging from the fashionable to the very kitsch. In these areas, from 10:00 p.m. to 2:00 a.m., the streets throng with young people hopping from one establishment to another. In Cuzco there are several foreign-owned "pubs" that attempt to assuage feelings of homesickness among weary travelers, as well as numerous bars and clubs.

Many restaurants include some form of live musical entertainment during the evening. For those really wanting to combine dining out with a musical experience, however, there is only one option: to head for a *peña*. Traditionally, a *peña* was a place where friends and neighbors got together to play folk music. In coastal cities they have evolved and, with input from the Afro-Peruvian community, they have become a popular form of weekend entertainment. In most cities there are a variety of types of *peña*, some specifically for tourists and others where members of the audience may suddenly leap up to sing or play an instrument such as the *cajón*.

THE CAJÓN

The *cajón* is a typically Peruvian percussion instrument. It consists of nothing more than a resonant wooden box, standing about 24 in (60 cm) high. Its origins go back to the mid-nineteenth century, when Black slaves tapped out rhythms on wooden fruit boxes. It has become the single most important and representative instrument of *musica criolla*. Internationally known exponents include Susana Baca and Novalima. Recently it has been incorporated into modern jazz, *nuevo* (new-style) flamenco, and Afro-Latin music. It is often accompanied by a donkey's jawbone, whose loosened teeth are rattled to the rhythm.

Most clubs also have live music, though each song can be, somewhat annoyingly, introduced, at length, by a compere. The music ranges from more traditional Colombian *salsa* and *cumbias*, to Peruvian *chicha*

and *tecno-cumbia*, as well as latin rap and hip-hop. A few *salsadromos* (*salsa* clubs), huge cavernous warehouse-type structures, still survive but many of these have become more flashy *discotecas*. Lima is now on the world tour itinerary of many internationally known musicians and rock groups.

SPORTS
Football

Football (soccer) is without doubt the sporting passion of Peruvians. The country would come to a stop if the national side were to play a truly important game, but the team has performed disappointingly for nearly thirty years and such occasions are a rarity. However, this doesn't prevent ordinary Peruvians from creating playing fields in the unlikeliest of locations, from deep in the jungle, to high-altitude mountainsides, to the floating reed islands of Lake Titicaca. One kick of the ball slightly too hard may bring a premature end to the game in all three cases, as may the distracting sight of a condor flying high above the pitches in the Colca Canyon.

Peru has rarely hit the headlines when it comes to football. In the 1978 World Cup, however, the Peruvian goalkeeper Ramon Quiroga— affectionately known as "El Loco" (the crazy one)— twice came to the attention of the world's media. In a group game with Poland he was immortalized as the first goalkeeper ever to receive a yellow card for a tackle inside the opposition half! In the final game of the second round, Argentina, the hosts, needed to

beat Peru by at least four goals to proceed to the quarter finals in place of Brazil. Argentina won 6–0 and went on to win the competition for the first time. The controversy surfaced when it was discovered that "El Loco" had been born in Argentina, though he wasn't blamed for conceding any of the goals. To this day the players and governments deny any conspiracy, but links between the two countries have always been strong. A few years later Peru was the only South American country to openly support Argentina in the Falklands War.

In Lima you will quickly need to decide whether you support Universitario ("La U"), the team of the educated *mestizo* supporters, or Alianza, that of the poorer Black populace. There is great rivalry between them—on a par with Manchester United versus Liverpool.

Other Sports

Aside from football the other popular national sport is volleyball: in the 1970s the Peruvian women's team was in the world's top five. Nets can be found on beaches, at recreos, and jungle lodges.

An increasing number of Peruvians and visitors are participating in adventure sports.

Surfing is popular among the young. The longest left-hand wave in the world can be found at Chicama, north of Trujillo, and national surfing championship events take place from beaches south of Lima to those in the far north. The 2004 women's world surfing champion was Peruvian.

Sandboarding is possible on dunes at several locations but is most exciting at the huge dunes surrounding the Huacachina oasis outside Ica.

Climbing and trekking are centered on Huaraz, for the Cordilleras Blanca and Huayahuash, and in the mountains around Cuzco. One of the most popular treks in the world is the Inca Trail, a three to four day trek from the Sacred Urubamba Valley to Machu Picchu.

White-water rafting is possible on the Cañete River, at Lunahuana, south of Lima, and on several Andean rivers, including the Urubamba and Colca.

Caballos de paso, Peruvian *paso* horses, are high stepping and elegant, a dream for those interested in equestrian dressage. Bred in Peru for more than four hundred years, they are now considered to be part of the national heritage. Trujillo and Lurin, south of Lima, are home to several stables and events.

Bull-fighting rings can be found in many Andean towns but the standard of bulls and matadors is often poor. Only in the Plaza de Acho, in Lima (July to October), can fights comparable to those found in Spain or Mexico be observed.

Many towns also have a *coliseo de gallos* where cockfighting can be viewed at close quarters.

CULTURAL ACTIVITIES

In terms of "Western" or high culture Peru is a bit of a backwater, though there are internationally recognized national orchestras and ballet companies in Lima. Furthermore, it has produced the likes of Juan Diego Flores, a current favorite at the Royal Opera House Covent Garden; Mario Testino, the celebrity portrait photographer; Luis Llosa, the Hollywood film director; and Frederick Ashton, founder of the English National Ballet, who grew up in Lima. A visit to a concert hall or the ballet in Lima will not disappoint.

CHABUCA GRANDA

The singer-composer Maria Isabel Granda Larco (1920–83) came from a conservative, privileged background. On divorcing, she became fascinated by Afro-Peruvian music and began composing and performing creole waltzes (*valses criollos*). Her behavior scandalized Lima society, but she was hugely popular among ordinary Peruvians and won international fame. Her two best-known songs, "Fina Estampa" and "La Flor de la Canela," are regularly performed by Latin American artists. She paved the way for Afro-Peruvian performers such as Susana Baca.

There are several noteworthy art museums, again in Lima, containing Italian art (Museo de Arte Italiano) and national art (Museo de Arte), including seventeenth- and eighteenth-century works of the Cuzco school of painting and more modern pieces. Aside from the museums, many banks in the major cities have their own private collections that open to the public: the Banco de Credito, in Lima, has several outstanding works by Zurbarán.

It is also well worth keeping an eye out for an exhibition of the work of the photographer Martin Chambi. Working in the first half of the twentieth century, out of a studio in Cuzco, he photographed not only the social elite but also the daily life of the Andean *campesinos*.

It is for literature that Peru has received the greatest international recognition. Among its luminaries are Cesar Vallejo (1892–1938), one of Latin America's foremost poets; Jose Maria Arguedas (1911–69), the anthropologist, linguist, and writer whose insights have made the Peruvian Indian world more clearly and widely understood; and Jose Carlos Mariategui (1894–1930), the journalist and social commentator whose reflections on Peruvian history and the plight of *campesinos* inspired many subsequent political groups, including APRA (see page 38) and various Peruvian Communist parties.

MARIO VARGAS LLOSA

Born in 1936, Peru's great novelist, playwright, essayist, journalist, and literary critic is one of Latin America's most venerated men of letters. Though Europe-based for much of his adult life, he has set almost all his works in Peru and exposed racial prejudice, violence, machismo, and corruption—common themes in Peruvian fiction. Some of his works also have a strong autobiographical thread, including one that describes his attempt to become President in 1990.

It is the literary quality of his work, however, rather than simply the subject matter that makes so much of it outstanding. Usually a good, if sometimes challenging, read, he typically employs multiple narrators, several concurrent stories, and flashbacks.

A prolific writer, arguably his most important works are *La Conversación en la Catedral* (*The Conversation in the Cathedral*, 1969), *La Tía Julia y el Escribidor* (*Aunt Julia and the Scriptwriter*, 1977), and *La Casa Verde* (*The Green House*, 1966). His work was further recognized in 2011 with the awarding of the Nobel Prize for Literature.

Now Peruvian cinema has also come to international attention with the films of Claudia Llosa such as *Made in USA* and *La Teta Asustada* (*The Milk of Sorrow*). The latter was nominated for a Best Foreign film Oscar in 2010.

SHOPPING FOR PLEASURE

The commercial centers of most towns are well stocked with a variety of goods but it is only in the really large cities that a very wide range can be found. Peru's own electronics and computer industries are no more, and now clothing and shoes are, increasingly, also imported from the Far East. Apart from visiting the main shopping streets there are a few major shopping centers in Lima, such as Larcomar in Miraflores, Jockey Plaza in Monterrico, and Camino Real in San Isidro, where Western goods can be found but the prices will only be particularly attractive in the sales (*rebajas*).

Visitors will find the handicraft markets to be of much greater interest. Most towns have a corner where shops, or stalls, sell mainly local products, ranging from food specialties, to knitwear, to jewelry, to elaborate woven textiles.
In Lima, however, handicrafts from all over the country can be found in vast covered markets such as Polvos Azules, in downtown Lima, and Avenida Petit Thouars, blocks 51–54, in Miraflores. The former is also the main "black market" outlet for goods in Lima. Handicrafts are no more expensive in most cases than in the areas where they are produced and it also saves carrying them all around the country with you on your travels. However, a greater choice and better quality may be found at the point of production.

Shopping in handicraft markets is not just a question of dashing in quickly and making an immediate purchase. Peruvian stallholders, even though they may make a huge effort to entice you to their own stall, expect you to visit other stalls to compare goods and prices. Be prepared to return several times to a stall, feign serious interest to begin with, bargain, and gradually bring the price down. It's all a bit of a game: a purchase should never be made at the initial price. A price reduction of a third to a half is quite possible.

HANDICRAFTS—WHAT TO BUY WHERE

Huancayo: silver jewelry, including fine filigree work.

Puno: alpaca and wool knitwear, especially distinctive on the islands of Tacquile and Amantani on Lake Titicaca.

Arequipa: high-quality alpaca and cotton knitwear.

Ayacucho: brightly painted model Nativity scenes in boxes (*retablos*), and woven wool wall hangings.

Cajamarca: elaborately painted mirrors.

Cuzco: knitwear, wall hangings, jewelry, wood carvings, and more.

Lima: *arpilleras*, appliqué pictures of Peruvian life made by women in shantytowns from cloth remnants. *Pima* (high-quality) cotton clothing and most other handicrafts.

Major credit cards can be used nationwide to make purchases in more upmarket hotels, shops, and restaurants, and to withdraw cash from ATMs, even in remoter towns.

While out shopping you may be approached by small children requesting a *propina* (gift); this also occurs at popular tourist sites. Their approach is usually fairly meek and mild but they can be persistent. Sometimes they will request an empty beer or soda bottle that they can recycle for cash but usually they ask for money. However, food, pens, or other useful items, rather than money or sweets, are also appropriate. In some circumstances they may offer to guide you in return for a small tip. If you don't wish to meet their demands then a firm "*No, gracias*" (No, thank you) will deter most.

TRAVELING

GETTING AROUND

Every long-distance journey in Peru is an adventure in itself. During the course of several hours you are likely to experience a range of landscapes, numerous culinary delicacies, and fluctuating degrees of comfort as the road surface or weather changes. This is particularly the case in the Andes, where, on a typical journey, you can expect to find guinea pigs or chickens around your feet, pass through some stunning scenery, be quizzed about football and politics, and watch an appalling movie. Peruvians are congenial travelers who like to engage their companions in conversation, when they aren't sleeping, and who will insist that the vehicle stops at the sight of a local food specialty offered at a roadside stall.

Air routes between all major cities usually provide a fast connection, though some flights, especially those involving jungle towns, are subject to weather delays. Almost all international flights land in Lima; a few from the USA and other South American countries fly directly into Cuzco and Arequipa. Apart from Lima there are about twenty major domestic airports. There are also numerous smaller landing strips in the Andes and Amazon where the terminal building may be little more than a corrugated-iron roofed hut.

Security at airports and bus terminals (now found in most cities) is good but care should always be taken in the surrounding streets. All major bus companies issue receipts for luggage placed in the hold or on the roof and some companies even take a photo and the fingerprints of travelers at the point of embarkation.

An extensive private bus network offers comprehensive national, interprovincial, and interurban services. On all major routes departures are surprisingly reliable and secure, but endless patience, snacks, playing cards, and a Walkman/Ipod may be useful on remote Andean journeys. On shorter (two hours) routes car "collectives" (*colectivos*) have now sprung up, offering a faster but slightly more expensive service.

Flying

Internal flights can drastically reduce travel times between major cities. However, because Lima acts as the domestic hub and many cities are only interconnected via Lima, it takes most of the day, for example, to travel from Cuzco to Iquitos.

There are no longer any Peruvian airlines operating internationally and this is also true on most domestic routes: LAN Peru (Chilean owned) offers the vast majority of flights, TACA (Costa Rican owned) and Peruvian Airlines (Peruvian owned) fly to Cusco, and there are several smaller Peruvian airlines serving remoter destinations.

Flights cost three to four times a first-class bus fare for the equivalent journey but take a fraction of the time. Foreign non-resident visitors are not entitled to purchase the discounted fares sometimes available on domestic flights. Around all national holidays and throughout July/August booking well in advance is essential and overbooking is a problem. This is also the case during local festivities, which vary from city to city. It is always advisable to arrive at the airport at least two hours before your flight.

Interprovincial Buses

On some routes National Express/Greyhound buses would find it hard to compete with the air-conditioning, satellite monitoring (for speed and security), leather-covered seats, three-course meals, and waitress service offered. On remoter Andean routes, however, thirty-year-old vehicles with cracked windows, holes in the floor, and belching fumes may be the only option.

Booking a couple of days in advance is advisable, if only to obtain a seat nearer the front or on the side of the bus with the best view. During national holidays and local festivals you should book a week in advance.

On the main coastal and some inland routes there are up to three standards of service: Executive (*Ejecutivo*), Economy (*Económico*), and Sleeper (*Bus Cama*), though different companies give them

different names. Executive is a nonstop service, comfortable, with onboard toilet and including a meal. Economy is the slower stopping service, more cramped and with a meal/toilet stop but about half the price of the Executive. *Bus Cama* operates at night, offering reclining seats and a service and price similar to the *Ejecutivo*.

In Lima the three main national companies, Civa, Cruz del Sur, and Ormeño, have terminals on Avenida Javier Prado Este. The offices of most of the other companies occupy several blocks where Avenida Paseo de la República enters downtown Lima. In most other cities there is either a terminal, sometimes quite far from the city center, or several blocks occupied by bus company offices, near the city center. In coastal cities there may be both northern and southern offices.

In the Andes it is a good idea to check with local people as to which company is currently the most reputable. Their buses should leave on time, be reasonably comfortable, and not too overloaded. Competing with them on shorter routes are *colectivos*—cars taking up to five passengers, so they are not necessarily more comfortable—which depart when full. They drive at high speed, take almost half the time of buses, but charge almost twice as much.

URBAN TRANSPORTATION

Most Peruvian cities are overrun with taxis. The official, registered taxis are usually painted yellow but there are many others operated by people trying to supplement their income. Taxis are cheap and

obliging, and the drivers are often prepared to discuss almost any topic. However, the small "Tico" make of taxi has a high accident rate and is best avoided. Always agree the fare before you get into the cab.

Municipal bus services in the largest cities are few and far between. Most urban public transportation is provided by *micros*: small buses; and *combis*: minibuses. They operate along fixed routes, but can be hailed and asked to stop almost anywhere along them. Most are uncomfortable, very crowded at peak times and, due to the frequent stops, very slow. Fares are fixed and low, so it's best to always carry some small change.

Given the unpredictability of drivers, always cross roads at official crossing points where these are indicated. A new law may make this a legal requirement.

TRAINS

Peru's once marvelous passenger rail network is in decline, with one exception—the spectacular Puno/Cuzco/Machu Picchu lines. Many lines in the north were destroyed in the 1970 earthquake, and significant improvements to the main roads have rendered the railways uncompetitive.

There is a daily service from Puno/Juliaca to Cuzco, and three tourist trains a day from Cuzco/Ollantaytambo to Machu Picchu. Despite the considerably faster highway running parallel to the tracks for much of its length, the journey by train between Cuzco and Puno is a must. Sadly, tourists are no longer allowed to travel in the same carriage as locals—gone are the days when you could sit around a table and play Casino with the local potato seed mafia—but are required to travel in expensive "special" trains. However, it's worth the experience for unrivaled vistas of the countryside, grazing herds of alpacas, small red-tiled villages, and a first glimpse of Lake Titicaca.

Machu Picchu can be reached only by train. These depart from both Cuzco and Ollantaytambo, in the Sacred Valley. There are two principal services: the "Vistadome" luxury service (carriages have glass roofs) includes food, and the "Backpacker." The latter stops at "Kilometer 88" to drop off those walking the Inca Trail to the ruins. Tourists are not allowed to travel on the local train service. All tickets must be purchased in advance.

THE HIGHEST RAILWAY IN THE WORLD

For those even vaguely interested in rail travel this is a once in a lifetime journey. In a little more than 60 miles (100 km) the central railway (Ferrocarril Central) climbs from sea level to nearly 15,750 feet (4,800 m) through gorges, past snowcapped peaks and lakes turned turquoise or red by mine workings, up to the city of Huancayo.

Engineered by a North American, Henry Meiggs, and constructed in the 1860s, the line is an incredible feat of engineering. It involves nearly sixty bridges, sixty-six tunnels, and over twenty switchbacks as it rises to cross the Andean watershed near Ticlio, the highest station in the world at 15,680 feet (4,782 m). In its heyday the service provided a three-course lunch and tea (as well as oxygen to those suffering from altitude sickness). The line is one of the great railway journeys of the world, but for the last twenty years it has, primarily, been open only to mine company trains. "Tourist Special" services operate occasionally.

There is a rustic passenger service between Huancayo and Huancavelica known as *el tren macho* because "it leaves when it wants and arrives when it can!" according to locals. In southern Peru the line from Mollendo to Arequipa, Juliaca, and Puno no longer operates a passenger service.

DRIVING

Driving in Peru is most definitely not for the fainthearted, either within urban areas or beyond, especially at night. In major towns the main arterial roads have reasonably good surfaces and are at least two lanes wide but still get very congested at peak times. The roads deteriorate away from the wealthier districts but even there the odd, sizable pothole is not uncommon.

Peruvian drivers love the sound of their horns, which beep incessantly as impatience is shown at every opportunity, especially when other drivers change lanes without warning  and nip into even the smallest space that may open up in front of them.

Traffic lights are respected in the daytime—major junctions are under the control of the traffic police: all women in smart uniforms—but at nighttime they are seen as little more than a recommendation. It is advisable to keep doors locked during urban journeys.

Special precautions need to be taken if driving in the Andes, particularly when leaving the few major highways. Adjustments may need to be made to the engine for the high altitude and additional fuel will need to be carried. In the Amazon some tools will be useful to extract your vehicle from the mud, though this may not prevent delays of several days in the rainy season.

The principal arterial road is the Panamericana highway running the length of the country, through the desert. It mainly consists of a single lane in each direction with no dividing barrier—accidents are common. Intermittently, sections are washed away or covered in drifting sand, necessitating a diversion. Only close to Lima is it of recognizable expressway standard. Every couple of hundred miles there are tolls (US $0.50–1.50 a vehicle), which become more frequent near Lima.

Several major roads run into the interior from the Panamericana. Many of these have been upgraded in the last few years but still consist of only a two-lane tarmac highway. All other roads are all-weather hard-core surfaced; the remoter they are, the worse their condition. Many Andean routes consist of a seemingly endless series of hairpin bends traversing the mountain ridges and valley sides: it can take half a day to cross from one valley to another.

There is only one decent, accurate road map: *Mapa Vial del Peru*, republished every five years. Regional road maps can also be obtained from the Touring & Automobile Club of Peru (Touring y Automóvil Club: www.touringperu.com.pe).

Fuel

Gas stations are run by Petroperú and international companies but are hard to find outside major urban areas, including along the Panamericana. Fuel of questionable quality can be obtained from informal roadside establishments. Unleaded (*sin plomo*) gasoline is widely available. Europeans will find fuel only slightly cheaper than at home.

Car Rental and Insurance

Peru does not yet have a road infrastructure that encourages car rental and touring vacations. There are a few car rental companies but most impose severe restrictions as to where the vehicle may be taken outside Lima. Furthermore, affordable insurance covers for only minor bumps and scrapes, and rental is restricted to those over twenty-five years old.

Speed Limits and Rules

Peruvian law requires vehicles to be roadworthy, for seat belts to be worn, and full documentation to be carried at all times. The speed limit in urban areas is 22–37 miles (35–60 km) per hour, depending on the urban zone, and on the Panamericana 62 miles (100 km) per hour. Only on the Panamericana do the police (Policía de Tránsito) deploy vehicles to enforce the limits and then only at certain locations. If you should be stopped, stay calm and, if they are in a good mood and you can humor them, you may avoid a fine. Fines are issued on a form (*papeleta*) and must be paid at Ministry of Transport offices, not direct to the policemen, though occasionally this approach may still work. In cities the female officers will not countenance an offer of on-the-spot payment for traffic offenses.

PARKING

Never leave your car parked unattended in the street. Outside better restaurants, clubs, and shops an official, or self-appointed, watchman will keep an eye on your vehicle for a small tip. Otherwise, use car lots (*playas de estacionamiento*), commonly known as *playas*, which charge up to US $1 per hour.

WHERE TO STAY

There is a wide range of accommodation in cities and major tourist areas, but in smaller towns and remoter regions the provision at the upper end is limited. At major holiday and festival times you are advised to book in advance. All but the most basic establishments will have a television in the room.

There are four categories of accommodation: *Hotel, Hotel Residencial, Hostal,* and *Pensión* or *Hospedaje*; all should identify themselves accordingly. A *hotel* is defined as having 50 plus rooms, while a *hostal* is smaller. Services, cleanliness, and prices should reflect this hierarchy but this isn't always the case. It is a good idea to check out the room, bathroom, and bed before agreeing to take the room. In most towns there is a significant amount of nighttime traffic so a room at the back may be preferable, though this can bring you closer to the dogs and chickens!

In coastal cities the top of the range hotels, often part of well-known chains, offer a full range of luxury hotel facilities. There are also some magnificent coastal villas in the far north and converted *haciendas* to retreat to in the valleys south of Lima. In the Andes, especially in the Cuzco, Sacred Valley, Cajamarca, and Colca Canyon environs there are many beautiful places of character, including converted monasteries, convents, and *haciendas*, in which to stay. They have often been  renovated to a high standard, with en suite facilities, fine dining rooms, and antique artifacts.

Mid-range *hotels/hostals* can be found everywhere but rarely have something special to recommend them. Often they are somewhat municipal in character but they are usually perfectly comfortable, clean, and friendly.

At the lower end there is a network of small *hospedajes* that have been "adopted" by backpackers and offer an ambience, services, and cafés to meet their needs. Here you are likely to meet up with fellow travelers on a regular basis over your muesli and fruit salad. Most cheaper places in the Andes have limited heating and can be very cold at night.

In the jungle most lodges provide a surprisingly good standard of accommodation, with three-course meals, comfortable beds, mosquito nets, running water, flush toilets, and rest areas strewn with hammocks. However, their prices can be comparable to a better hotel.

Camping is growing in popularity among Peruvians and in popular coastal and trekking areas there are basic campsites where a small fee is levied.

 Elsewhere camping is at your own risk. Care should be taken if camping near to settlements of any size—it may be best to seek permission from someone of responsibility within the community to reduce the risk of pilfering—and with respect to sites that might be subject to flooding or landslides.

HEALTH

In urban areas there are plenty of pharmacies (*farmacias*) and *boticas*; the latter once produced their own remedies and are more common in rural areas. Pharmacists can often assist with minor health matters if your communication skills are up to it. In major cities the pharmacies and boticas operate a night rota system. Most medication that requires a prescription in the UK also requires one in Peru. Bring any prescribed medicine with you, if possible. The cost of medicine in Peru is similar to the USA, though older drugs that may no longer be sold in the US are cheaper. Compared to the UK, some drugs are cheaper but most are more expensive. Keep an eye on the expiration dates.

It is a good idea to carry a small first-aid kit, and if spending time in a remote area, you could consider purchasing a specialist traveler's medical pack. Water purification tablets should also be brought for such trips, while only bottled or boiled water should be drunk at all other times.

The sun is extremely strong, given Peru's proximity to the equator. Suntan lotion, sunglasses, and a hat are essential if spending time outdoors anywhere, including at altitude in the Andes. Sunbathing on the coast should not be considered without protection and for only a couple of hours at a time, even with sunscreen.

Contact lens solution and spare contacts or glasses should be brought, as necessary.

Vaccinations

No vaccinations are required before entering Peru but it's a good idea to have the following:

Polio/tetanus: boosters give at least ten years' coverage.

Typhoid: three years' coverage.

Rabies: a double jab, six months apart, gives five

years' protection. Strongly recommended if going off the beaten track.

Hepatitis A and B: recommended if eating in remoter areas in establishments with uncertain hygiene standards.

Yellow fever: much of Peru is a designated risk area. Free vaccinations are given, if arriving by plane, at the airport in the three major jungle towns: Iquitos, Pucallpa, and Puerto Maldonado.

Malaria: a potential threat in the Amazon region below 8,200 feet (2,500 m). However, the risk is greater in the north than the south, where many short-term visitors opt not to take medication.

Rabies occurs in Peru and care should be taken approaching domesticated animals. If heading off the beaten track it is a good idea to be vaccinated against rabies before traveling. In the jungle rabies is endemic in many species, so think twice about stroking lodge "pets." However, the incidence level is low and most Peruvians do not worry about it.

Seek specialist medical advice from your doctor or a vaccination center prior to departure. If staying longer in the jungle, ask about dengue fever, Chagas' disease, and leishmaniasis.

Health Insurance

Excellent health care can be found in Lima's private hospitals but there are few in the other major cities. The state system is extremely variable, though there will be at least a limited provision in remoter towns. Often the expertise of the staff there is not matched by the facilities or the medications available. Travel insurance is essential. If you fall seriously ill, rapid evacuation to Lima is probably the best option.

NATURAL HAZARDS

Altitude Sickness (soroche)

Any journey into the mountains above 10,000 feet (3,050 m) carries a risk, especially if undertaken rapidly. Few travelers are seriously affected and a day of rest and plenty of liquid—*coca* leaf tea (*mate de coca*), not alcohol—helps most people. If symptoms of nausea, tiredness, and severe headaches persist beyond a couple of days, seek medical advice immediately: a return to a lower altitude may be necessary. If you are planning a trekking or climbing trip, at least two to three days acclimatizing at around 10,000 feet is advisable before going higher.

Earth Tremors

These occur frequently, particularly along the coast and in the Andes, but devastating earthquakes are rare. The last occurred in 1970 and killed 30,000, but in 2007 a big quake hit the coastal town of Pisco killing nearly 600 and affecting over 400,000. Most modern public buildings have been designed to withstand quakes. If you are caught in a tremor, or quake, evacuate immediately to a designated place within the building or to an open area outside. Older buildings are most likely to fail.

Communications may be disrupted for some time after the event, especially if it has triggered landslides and blocked roads.

Flooding

A constant hazard in the Amazon basin and, at times, in the Andes, washing away bridges and roads, but vehicles invariably still manage to find a way through. Arguably, landslides, resulting from flooding and tremors, pose a greater threat to the infrastructure and so to travel itineraries.

"El Niño"/"La Niña"

These do not occur on an annual basis. However, a severe "El Niño" is likely to occur every ten years; the last significant one was in 1998, causing major damage and disruption to the north coast. Travelers are likely to be inconvenienced only after the event by infrastructure damage. If in the area at the height of the storms, you would be strongly advised to move inland and away from anywhere likely to be subject to flash floods.

The "La Niña" phenomenon mainly affects the southern *sierra*, including the Arequipa region. Travelers passing through at this time need to be prepared for extremely low temperatures, especially at night—time to put on that thick alpaca jumper!

SAFETY

Peru is, broadly, a safe country to travel in. However, as in most countries, there are places to be avoided, valuables should not be flaunted, and lone travelers should take special care. Travelers should try to ensure that they know where they are going before they set out—avoid standing on street corners looking lost and retreat into a shop, or church, to check your bearings if necessary. Local people will often indicate if you stray into a dangerous area and help you if something has gone wrong.

SENSIBLE PRECAUTIONS

- Poorer districts of all towns and cities should be avoided, including during the day. At night, stick to well-lit streets in the city center or take a taxi.
- Possessions of any value should be kept, preferably hidden, in internal pockets and belts. Try not to carry valuables in bags and never leave bags unattended. Lock valuables away in a bag in all but the top hotels.
- Petty criminals use a variety of methods to distract and rob travelers. Walk quickly away from any stranger who tries to attract your attention in a suspicious manner. If robbed, do not pursue the thief as they often work with hidden accomplices.
- In major tourist centers there are specialist tourist police. Contact them immediately, if only to obtain the appropriate insurance claim paperwork. In Lima, the Tourist Police (Policía de Turismo) contact number is 01.423.3500.
- Around town and for short journeys it is not necessary to carry your passport on you, if it can be left safely somewhere.

PLACES TO VISIT
Lima

Many travelers do not give the "City of Kings" the chance to live up to its name, and some even pass straight through. Lima, however, is a fascinating and dynamic city, surviving against the odds in the driest desert on earth, and it is at the center of most of what goes on in Peru. It is vast, restricted to the narrow coastal plain, but extending over 30 miles (50 km) north to south. Most visitors will confine themselves to the historic core, known as "downtown Lima," and the coastal suburbs of Miraflores and Barranco, famed for their shopping and nightlife respectively. Fine baroque monasteries and colonial houses, with ornate carved balconies, are scattered liberally across downtown Lima, a UNESCO World Heritage Site. The Barrio Chino offers some of the best Chinese cuisine in South America.

In Miraflores a thriving café society, handicrafts markets, and boutiques attract shoppers. The fishing village of Barranco is now the hub for cool bars, clubs, and more traditional *peñas*, showing signs of life only after 9:00 p.m.

Lima also contains some superb museums, including the Gold Museum (Museo de Oro), in Monterrico; National Museum (Museo de la Nación), in San Borja; and Archaeology and Anthropology Museum (Museo de Archaeología y Anthropología), in Pueblo Libre. However, if erotic pottery is your thing then head for the Larco Herrera Museum, in Pueblo Libre, or for ancient textiles the Amano Museum, in Miraflores. And then there is the Parque de la Reserva with the largest fountain show in the world, enhanced by music and lights, and best viewed in the evening.

Outside Lima

Peru has a vast wealth of natural, pre-Columbian, Inca, and colonial attractions. The challenge for most travelers is to decide what to see in the average three- to four-week trip. The challenge for Peru is to improve the infrastructure and persuade them to visit some of the less well-known but equally wonderful sites elsewhere.

Major natural attractions include the Cotahausi and Colca canyons, the two deepest in the world; Gocta, the second highest waterfall in the world; Lake Titicaca, the highest navigable lake in the world; the beautiful Sacred Valley of the Incas; the magnificent Cordilleras Blanca and Huayhuash, ideal for trekking and climbing; the long sandy beaches of the far north, deserted for much of the year; and, last but not least, the superb wildlife of the Amazon rain forest.

The most significant pre-Columbian sites are located in the coastal valleys. Arguably the most fascinating are the Nasca Lines—best viewed from the air. Most other major sites are in the north, including Caral; the Huacas del Sol y de la Luna and Chan-Chan, near Trujillo; and the adobe pyramids of Sipan, Batan Grande, and Tucume, near Chiclayo. They all have reasonable visitor infrastructures. The awe-inspiring ruins of Chavin, Huamachuco, and Kuelap, in the northern Andes, are fabulous.

However, it is the Inca sites that are the most photogenic and attract most interest, most notably the "lost city of the Incas:" Machu Picchu. In the Sacred Valley the ruins at Pisac and Ollantaytambo

are extremely impressive, while the less visited, more overgrown, and atmospheric sites along the Inca Trail to Machu Picchu and at Choquequirao are recommended if you are feeling adventurous.

Aside from "downtown" Lima the city centers of several other towns and cities contain well-preserved colonial buildings, including Arequipa (built from white volcanic rock, *sillar*), Trujillo (brightly painted mansions surround the main plaza), Cuzco (many built on top of Inca foundations), and Ayacucho (most evident in the ecclesiastical architecture).

Indigenous culture is widely in evidence throughout the Andes but especially in the south around Cuzco, the Colca valley, and across the *altiplano* approaching and along the shores of Lake Titicaca. In these places it is possible to pick up a strong Indian flavor through their markets, costumes, and frequent *fiestas*.

chapter eight

BUSINESS BRIEFING

BUSINESS CULTURE

Personal relationships are the absolute key to most business deals in Peru. A degree of formality and good manners is expected but so is a more personal approach that will lead to mutual trust and respect. The establishment of a business relationship is rarely achieved over the phone—Peruvians do business in person, not at a distance. After discussions around the table Peruvians will also expect there to be a degree of socializing. Networking and social skills are vital in establishing business relationships in Peru.

Status and Hierarchy

Most businesses in Peru are very hierarchical, with top management making many of the more mundane decisions than might be expected in a Western company. With decisions passing through several management levels, expect answers and decisions to take time. Additional time will also be required if attempting to do business with local branches of banks and other institutions because decisions may need to be referred back to the Lima head office.

Connections

Nepotism was rife in Peruvian business until recently. The family name, ethnicity, schooling, university background, and whether you grew up in Lima or the provinces, played crucial roles in securing employment. Nowadays, with a growing percentage of top executives having studied abroad, especially in the USA, this approach is changing. The increasing number of foreign employers has also encouraged the switch to a meritocracy. However, family contacts can still be important lower down the career ladder.

Addressing and Greeting People

Peruvians, as in most Hispanic countries, use three names: their first name, followed by their father's surname, and then their mother's surname. All three appear on most business cards but the second surname may be abbreviated to an initial. Only use the first surname when addressing people.

Peruvians also place great store by their professional qualifications and titles: it reflects both their level of education and seniority within a company. Don't refer to a professional contact simply as *Señor* or *Señora*. For example, an engineer will be introduced as *ingeniero(a)*, an architect as *arquitecto(a)*, and a doctor as *doctor(a)*. A skilled craftsman such as a carpenter or plumber will often be called *maestro*, confirming his status and your trust in him.

When greeting people physically a handshake is mandatory on meeting and saying good-bye to business contacts. As familiarity grows then a pat or two on the shoulder following a handshake would be quite normal between two Peruvian 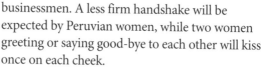 businessmen. A less firm handshake will be expected by Peruvian women, while two women greeting or saying good-bye to each other will kiss once on each cheek.

Business Style
Peruvians dress formally in the office and for business meetings appearance is important. You should do likewise and, if in doubt, dress on the

conservative side. Men are expected to wear a suit and tie but in summer a short sleeve shirt is acceptable and jackets can be removed. For women a formal suit, dress, skirt, or smart trousers, depending on the season, are the norm.

In summer, when it is very hot, remember that most offices have air-conditioning and can be on the chilly side. In the absence of air-conditioning, it is not acceptable to remove your jacket and roll up your sleeves unless in an informal meeting.

Expect initial business meetings to be quite formal until a working relationship and confidence are established. First impressions are important, so you should know a few appropriate words, or phrases, in Spanish to greet and address your hosts (see below). Overall, once you are involved in a business partnership you will find the Peruvian business style friendly and relaxed.

Women in Business
Machismo is very much alive and well in Peru but the number of women active in business is on the increase. In the business context women are likely to be treated with the utmost respect, accepted as equals, and shown a degree of old-fashioned courtesy typical of a male-dominated society.

When it comes to entertainment foreign businesswomen will usually be invited to lunch rather than to dinner. This would also be the case if your Peruvian business partner is a woman.

Business Hours

Working hours depend on the nature of the business. Industrial employees usually start work early at 8:00 a.m. and finish by 5:00 p.m. They often also work Saturdays, 8:30 a.m. to 1:00 p.m. Office hours are generally 8:30 a.m. to 5:30 p.m., with lunch taken between 1:00 and 2:00 p.m.

Bank hours vary around the country, from 9:00 a.m. to 6:00 p.m. in Lima, while outside Lima they close for lunch, commonly 1:00 to 3:00 p.m. In Lima and Cuzco banks may also be open from 9:00 a.m. to 1:00 p.m. on Saturdays. Expect long lines for changing money and business-related matters.

MAKING APPOINTMENTS

Appointments are best made by phone, especially for a first meeting, but e-mail is being used increasingly. Special notice should be taken of public, religious, and local holidays, while Friday afternoons are not usually an opportune time.

In most large companies receptionists and secretaries will speak some English. However, it may be advisable to have some phrases in Spanish on hand or a Spanish speaker to call upon. If you can establish a good relationship with the secretary, your chances of making contact with the boss will be improved. Despite Peruvians being poor timekeepers, foreign visitors will be expected to be on time for business meetings, though it is not uncommon to then be kept waiting—occasionally you may arrive for a meeting only to find that your counterparts have changed their schedule or itinerary.

BUSINESS MEETINGS

In general, business meetings in Peru are fairly informal affairs. There is not usually an agenda but points for discussion may be agreed upon at the start of the meeting. This is done among those attending rather than by appointing a chairman. During the meeting anyone present may contribute who has valid point to make—there is no question of following rank.

Minutes will rarely be taken: each attendee makes their own notes regarding matters that relate to their responsibilities. When complex technical matters are discussed then an *acta de reunion* (record of the meeting) may be prepared afterwards and signed by all parties.

PRESENTATIONS

A presentation should always begin with the
focus on the team leader but once up and running
attention should also be given to other team
members—Peruvian managers like to involve
everyone. At a first meeting a presentation is best
kept short and to the point, with a clear summary
at the end of the main points that need,
subsequently, to be discussed/negotiated.
Peruvians will appreciate a professional
presentation with clear graphics and illustrations:
make a bit of a "song and dance" but not too
much. In subsequent meetings more precise
information, including detailed facts and figures,
can be presented.

The most important thing to get across is that
your business proposal is serious, that you can
supply what you promise, and that you have
strong backup (financial, staffing, etc.) to support
it: this will create trust among Peruvian
counterparts. They will also greatly appreciate
your proposal if presented as one of "partnership"
rather than as a simple supplier–customer
relationship. Furthermore, their preference will
be for arrangements that, from the beginning,
are perceived as long term.

NEGOTIATIONS

The patriarchal nature of society, combined with
increasingly Western business acumen, requires a

direct approach to negotiations. Most tricky are family-run businesses (there are many in Peru) where the family member in charge will, initially, have to be convinced of the proposal's merits. If the business has risen from humble beginnings then a useful tactic is to make them feel that they originated the final proposals.

Price negotiations should commence at realistic levels, not greatly overinflated, and there should be some leeway to reduce prices as the negotiations progress. Peruvians are keen on flexibility and will want you to adopt a similar approach rather than arriving with fixed conditions and prices. A compromise solution at the end of negotiations will be expected.

Remember that the economy is growing and a Peruvian company will be looking for the best deal available. Consequently, negotiations can take time and both partners need to be direct, but as soon as an acceptable deal is made expect matters to come to a quick conclusion.

GIFT GIVING

Gifts are only exchanged with business associates on Independence Day (July 28) and at Christmas; a company product or promotional item is a common gift. Other appropriate gifts are imported goods such as whiskey, wine, chocolates, and leather goods (bags and wallets are popular) rather than Peruvian products, apart from a good quality

bottle of *pisco*. When the
businessperson from
abroad is doing the
giving, something from
your own country will
be well received, or one
of your company's own
promotional gifts.

The gift should not be
from the cheaper end of the range available but
then again it need not normally be something
extravagant. Much depends on the nature of the
individual business relationship and, with time,
more personal, specially chosen gifts would be in
order.

"FAVORS"

As we have seen, large-scale corruption has
reached the highest political office in recent years.
Day-to-day business, however, is not overtly
corrupt and Peru is by no means the worst in
Latin America in this respect. Peruvian law should
ensure transparency in all business deals. Such
"corruption" as does exist is the by-product of a
hierarchical, patronage-based society and in most
cases is based on "favors" rather than payments.
A few "favors" grease the wheels and help
maintain useful contacts when doing business or
dealing with bureaucracy in Peru. In this respect,
you may need to rely on your business contact

having family members, or friends, working in local government or customs, for example, who can be called upon to assist, if required.

BUSINESS ENTERTAINMENT

As we have seen, Peruvians love to dine out and business entertainment often involves a visit to a restaurant. If you are a vegetarian or have special dietary needs then you will need to find a way to convey this because most Peruvians will assume that you are a meat/fish eater. It goes without saying that your host will cover the cost of all the entertainment.

A lunch will be seen as an opportunity to continue business discussions and not purely as a social occasion, though some nonbusiness related chat is a good idea. Talks over dinner are likely to begin with business matters but as the evening wears on it will become a more social occasion. Socializing in the evening, especially for a visitor from abroad, could also involve a visit to a piano/cocktail bar or a *peña*. This will be seen much more as an occasion to get to know each other rather than an extension of the business meeting. When Peruvians go out to enjoy themselves they don't like to bring work with them. However, this is an opportunity to find other areas of common interest that may help to sustain the business relationship.

In terms of conversation, remember that Peruvians are extremely patriotic and also love their hometown. So, for example, a Limeño (person from Lima) would rarely say anything too critical about the city or its people. You should follow suit, even if the pollution levels that day are terrible and your taxi ride in from the airport lengthy.

Business breakfasts are quite common and occur when there is no other opportunity to meet. They usually take place early, 8–9:00 a.m. at the latest, and are sharp, to the point affairs. Go with your paperwork and be prepared to spread it out all across the table among the *chicharrones*, *camote frito* (fried sweet potato), and coffee.

Business lunches are usually held quite early, commonly 12:00–1:00 p.m., or 1:00–2:00 p.m. They are also fairly quick events, lasting little more than an hour despite the fact that lunch is usually the main meal—such are the pressures of the working day. Lunch is an important occasion to cement a relationship and confirm that doing business together would be a good idea.

Business dinners are reserved more for visitors from abroad. Peruvians doing business together would rarely entertain each other unless they had become personal friends. If you are alone then your business contacts will certainly not countenance the idea of you dining alone or retiring early to your hotel room. Given the business schedule that you will be expected to keep to, combined with the likely entertainment arrangements, a business visit to Peru is more suited to the insomniac and the late-to-bed individual. A business dinner, or visit to a bar, is unlikely to commence prior to 8:00 p.m. and could easily go on until close to midnight, even if you have a 7:00 a.m. start the next day.

EMPLOYMENT FOR FOREIGNERS

Unless you work for a transnational company or a charity and are posted to Peru there are few formal employment opportunities.

Lima has many foreign language schools—at least six major schools teach entirely through the medium of English—and opportunities arise from time to time for teachers in these institutions. Otherwise, English language schools in major towns around the country may have openings every so often but this will be temporary employment on a local wage.

A few jungle lodges employ graduate biologists as guides but as more Peruvian biologists gain language skills the number of opportunities is declining. There are very limited possibilities for those with specialist climbing, rafting, or outdoor skills with adventure tour companies.

A business visa is required by foreigners if employed by a Peruvian company: they will arrange it. Paid employment is not permitted on a tourist visa (90-day limit). Foreign employees are respected for their skills: it's an opportunity for a two-way exchange.

CONTRACTS AND FULFILLMENT

Business contracts follow El Codigo Civil Peruano (Peruvian Civil Code), which is based on the Roman legal system adapted to Peruvian circumstances. A contract, normally, covers all aspects of the business agreement and its drawing up is overseen by a lawyer. In Peru contracts must be written in Spanish, so you may need to request a translation. Covering all aspects of the deal in the contract means it is rare for contracts to be broken or renegotiated, though there is some flexibility for minor amendments by mutual agreement. Business preliminaries with a private company may commence prior to the contract signature but within the state sector the signing must be awaited.

If a disagreement arises then the correct course of action is to resort to law or arbitration. Failure to complete a contract on time will, usually, incur a daily penalty, which is written into the contract.

All business activity in Peru involves a significant volume of official paperwork. However, your Peruvian business partners will be only too willing to advise you in this respect and see that you successfully negotiate the bureaucratic nightmare of customs forms, tax payments, and so forth.

Any business deal in Peru is more likely to be successful with good employee management. The boss still makes most decisions in the office but, increasingly, staff are consulted on matters that concern them. Bosses are expected to show some interest in the families of close employees but it does not mean that he or she should be intrusive. A casual concern will be expected, rather than no concern, to ensure good employee relations.

Many areas of the economy are unionized in both the public and private sectors. Strikes are not uncommon, despite loss of pay and the risk of losing their job, as workers try to improve their conditions.

chapter nine

COMMUNICATING

LANGUAGE
Spanish is the first official language
of Peru, and the first language of
the majority of Peruvians. It is the
second most widely spoken language
on earth. Despite variations in
accent, dialect, and local vocabulary,
a Spanish speaker will always be
understood in another Spanish-
speaking country. While non-Spanish
speakers are limited in the experiences they could
derive from a visit to Peru, even a few words of
Spanish can make all the difference in certain
circumstances.

Spanish—the Peruvians prefer to call it
Castellano—was originally a dialect spoken in
Castile and Leon in northern Spain in the twelfth
century. It stems from Latin but incorporates
many words from other languages, especially
Arabic from the period of Spain's occupation by
the Moors. By the fifteenth century it was the
language of the Spanish court and, consequently,
the language of the Conquest.

In Peru Castellano has evolved differently from the Spanish of Spain. It has retained traditional words and expressions from the time of the Conquest, and incorporates words adopted from Quechua and other indigenous languages.

The language used in Peru is more formal, so you should always address someone you don't know well using the *usted/ustedes* form for "you" and not the more familiar *tu/vosotros* form.

Quechua words are used for many indigenous products such as grains (*quinoa* and *kiwicha*); or animals (*vicuña, llama,* and *condor*); *poncho* is also a Quechua word, while *alpaca* is an Aymara word. Many indigenous place-names, some from pre-Columbian cultures, survive. There are also Latin American Spanish words that are not used within Spain, such as *palta* (avocado, *aguacate* in Spain) or words with double meaning such as *castaña* (chestnut in Spain but Brazil nut in Peru).

One major difference in spoken Spanish is the pronunciation of the letter "c" when it is followed by a soft vowel (e or i), or a "z" followed by any vowel. In both cases in Spain they are pronounced as the English "th," while in Peru they are pronounced as a soft "c." For example, the word for "beer," spelled *cerveza,* would be pronounced as *thervetha* in Spain but *cerveca* in Peru.

Speaking Spanish

Spanish is relatively straightforward for an English speaker to learn. Peruvians are always enthusiastic when visitors show that they can speak some Spanish and it will assist greatly in developing friendships. Most Peruvians will be patient if you speak only broken Spanish and have a limited vocabulary. In major tourist areas, especially Lima and Cuzco, there will be locals who speak at least some English. However, outside these areas and in all remote areas a working knowledge of Spanish is essential.

Café Pasado

In Peru, if you want a cup of drip (filter) coffee then ask the waiter for *café pasado*—coffee that has passed through a filter. However, in Spain or Mexico, if you ask for *café pasado* they will give you a strange look. "Don't you want fresh coffee, today's coffee (*café de hoy*)?," they will inquire!

One thing to remember is that Spanish speakers don't generally say "please" (*por favor*) and "thank you" (*gracias*) as much as English speakers. A direct translation of a request for something may come across as quite abrupt, almost rude, with no "please" or "thank you" attached to it, but no offense is meant. If you choose to be very polite then you may find yourself ridiculed or taken to be someone from a humble background.

Another characteristic of Castellano not found in Spain is the use of diminutives and aliases.

Peruvians love to call each other names, so someone called John may well be known by family and friends as Joncito, while, if he is tall and thin, his friends may call him Flaco (slim).

Other Languages

Many other languages are spoken in Peru: Quechua, the second official language, and Aymara. Both are spoken in the *sierra*, the former widely, though there are numerous dialects, and the latter around Lake Titicaca. In the Amazon there are many indigenous languages, some spoken by several thousand and others, now, by just a handful of individuals. In remoter areas older people and some women many not speak Spanish, though children, through their schooling, will be bilingual. In these areas Spanish may be very much people's second language.

FACE-TO-FACE

When two male friends meet they normally shake hands and pat each other's shoulders. Two women friends meeting would kiss once on each cheek, as would a man and a woman. The first verbal exchange is usually an inquiry about the other's health—how are you? (*¿Cómo estás?* / *¿Qué tal?*)— before moving on to other topics.

Peruvians like to talk, often with the volume turned up, and accompany their comments with animated gesticulations. However, they are quieter, softer in their manner, and less aggressive than the Spanish. Peruvians laugh easily and like to make a joke out of almost any situation.

They have no problem making eye contact and will consider it strange if you don't during a conversation or discussions, but, in public, women should avoid direct eye contact with passing men. Similarly, a degree of body contact in passing in the street or on public transportation would not be considered overtly aggressive but might be considered provocative if a woman brushes against a man. In the past, in "downtown" areas, it was not unknown for women to suffer unsolicited personal contact. This is now less common.

ENGLISH-LANGUAGE PUBLICATIONS

Rumbos is an on-line magazine promoting culture and tourist destinations in Peru. In the center of Miraflores, in Lima, and in Cuzco it is possible to pick up *Time* and *Newsweek*, plus copies of *The Times* (London and New York), *International Herald Tribune*, and some other foreign titles, a few days old. Outside Lima and Cuzco this is almost impossible.

SERVICES
Mail
The postal system is called Serpost. Main post offices (Correo Central) are open from 8:00 a.m.

to 6:00 p.m., Monday to Friday, and from 9:00 to 12:00 a.m. on Saturdays.

Most post offices offer a mail-holding service. Letters should be addressed to the recipient (surname first) at Posta Restante, followed by the name of the town and the department. Remember that for surnames starting with a "W," mail will probably be placed in the "V" section, as there is no letter "W" in Spanish. You will need to show ID when picking items up.

The Peruvian postal service cannot be relied on. When sending post insist that you actually see your mail franked or with stamps stuck on it: do not pay if you are told that this will be done later. Post boxes (*el buzon*) are always inside post offices.

The mail service is also expensive, especially for larger items and parcels. Even a postcard to Europe or North America costs $1. For personal correspondence the proliferation of Internet cafés provides a faster and more cost-effective option.

Parcels are best sent using a courier company such as DHL or Federal Express but they only have offices in Lima and a few cities.

Telephone

Since the network was sold to Telefónica, of Spain, the service has improved and this has also led to the expansion of the Internet. Pay phones have proliferated and can be found even in small towns. They all operate with prepurchased phone cards, but even local calls are expensive.

Peru's country code is 51. Most numbers have 8 digits, combining the area code and local number. In Lima add a 1 prefix to the number; all other area codes are two digit. When dialing out of Peru, dial 00 followed by the country code. For directory inquiries dial 108; for the operator, 100.

Cell phones are being used increasingly in Peru. Cell phone calls are now cheaper than land line calls (although land line calls are still cheaper than in the USA). Cell phones have become more affordable, and there are different types of deals and tariffs. The two main network providers are Telefónica Movistar and Claro. Telefónica has the most comprehensive coverage but Claro is dominant in some areas. On arriving in Peru it is best to check which network is most active where you are going to be based and which is used by your contacts

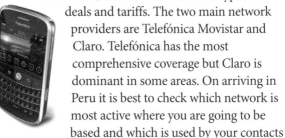

before subscribing. Inter-network communication is expensive so many Peruvian businessmen own two phones, one for each network. Most European phones can be easily activated on the purchase of an appropriate chip. All cell phone numbers in Peru begin with the prefix 9. When answering the phone Peruvians commonly say "*Alo*" ("Hello") or "*Digame*" ("Speak to me"), and then wait for your response.

Internet
Internet cafés can be found in most towns. The quality and speed of the machines is often not

great and, in the remoter towns, a continuous network connection is not guaranteed. However, they are cheap, typically charging $1 per hour.

Most Peruvians in urban areas now have a Facebook page and use it as a regular means of communication to overcome distance, especially with friends and relatives living in other cities and abroad.

CONCLUSION

A popular saying in Peru states: "*Este es el país de las maravillas*" ("This is the land of marvels"). The visitor will quickly discover that this phrase doesn't apply only to its spectacular topography, incredible biodiversity, and amazing ancient remains but also to its hospitable and friendly people. Peruvians welcome visitors, though in rural areas they may remain a bit wary. The phrase also signifies that in Peru almost anything is possible and usually it is!

The family lies at the heart of Peruvian society, a constant source of pleasure and support. Only the Catholic Church earns similar respect. It is also the chief unifying force in a country containing tremendous cultural diversity, reflected in its festivals and *fiestas*.

Business travelers are welcome, especially if they show flexibility, a personal touch, and the ability to enjoy life beyond the workplace. Your

Peruvian counterparts are likely to be extremely hospitable and interested in you as an individual. Once you get to know each other and value the relationship, your business venture will have a good chance of succeeding.

Whatever your reasons for visiting, knowing more about Peru's culture will both deepen your experience and help you to have realistic expectations. Witnessing the hardships faced by many Peruvians on a daily basis is unavoidable, but you will also discover that they are a stoical, hardworking, optimistic, and sociable people with a great capacity for enjoyment and finding humor in life whenever possible.

Further Reading

Alden Mason, John. *The Ancient Civilizations of Peru*. London: Penguin, 1991.

Bingham, Hiram. *Lost City of the Incas*. London: Weidenfeld & Nicolson, 2001.

Box, Ben. *Peru Guide*. Bath: Footprint, 2011.

Crabtree, John. *Peru: An Oxfam Country Profile*. Oxford: Oxfam, 2002.

Hemming, John. *Conquest of the Incas*. London: Pan, 2004.

Heyerdahl, Thor. *Pyramids of Tucume: the Quest for Peru's Forgotten City*. London: Thames & Hudson, 1995.

Holligan, Jane. *Peru in Focus*. London: Latin American Bureau, 1998 / New York: Interlink Books, 1998.

Jenkins, Dilwyn. *Rough Guide to Peru*. London: Rough Guides Ltd, 2009.

Kendall, Ann. *Everyday Life of the Incas*. London: Batsford, 1978.

Milligan, Max. *Realm of the Incas*. London: Harper Collins, 2001.

Poole, Deborah, and Gerardo Rénique. *Peru: Time of Fear*. London: Latin American Bureau, 1992.

Thomson, Hugh. *The White Rock*. London: Phoenix/Orion Books, 2003.

Tickell, James and Oliver. *Cuzco, Peru*. London: Tauris Parke, 1989.

Vargas Llosa, Mario. *The Greenhouse*, and numerous other novels and plays.

Wright, Ronald. *Cut Stones and Crossroads*. London: Penguin, 1984.

Various. *Peru Reader: History, Culture and Politics*. Durham, North Carolina: Duke University Press, 2006.

Spanish. A Complete Course. New York: Living Language, 2005.

In-Flight Spanish. New York: Living Language, 2001.

Fodor's Spanish for Travelers (CD Package). New York: Living Language, 2005.

Index

Acknowledgments

We would like to thank Luisa Granda Luján and Enrique Beingolea Barua for their invaluable help and expertise in researching this book.